THE AMAZING STORY
OF THE MAN WHO CYCLED
FROM INDIA TO
EUROPE FOR
LOVE

PER J ANDERSSON

Translated by
ANNA HOLMWOOD

ONEWORLD

A Oneworld book

First published in North America, Great Britain and Australia
by Oneworld Publications, 2017
This mass market paperback edition published 2017

Originally published in Swedish as *New Delhi – Borås*
by Forum, 2014

ISBN 978-1-78607-208-5
ISBN 978-1-78607-034-0 (eBook edition)

Printed and bound in Great Britain by Clays Ltd, St Ives plc

Two images on p.296 © PA Images

Oneworld Publications
10 Bloomsbury Street
London WC1B 3SR
England

Stay up to date with the latest books,
special offers, and exclusive content from
Oneworld with our monthly newsletter

Sign up on our website
oneworld-publications.com

Contents

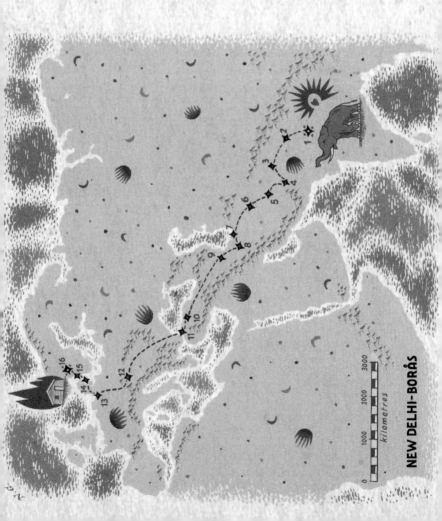

1 New Delhi, India
2 Amritsar, India
3 Kabul, Afghanistan
4 Kandahar, Afghanistan
5 Herat, Afghanistan
6 Mashhad, Iran
7 Sari, Iran
8 Tehran, Iran
9 Tabriz, Iran
10 Ankara, Turkey
11 Istanbul, Turkey
12 Vienna, Austria
13 Hamburg, Germany
14 Copenhagen, Denmark
15 Gothenburg, Sweden
16 Borås, Sweden

NEW DELHI–BORÅS

0   1000   2000   3000
kilometres

The Prophecy

*E*ver since the day I was born, in a village in the Indian jungle, my life course has been steered by a prophecy.

It was winter and almost time for the New Year celebrations, which remained a tradition, even though the British who had introduced them to our country had left two years earlier. It rarely rained in December, but that year the north-eastern monsoon lingered on the Orissa coast. Eventually the rain subsided, but the forested slopes on either side of the river remained hidden in the dark clouds that doused the landscape in twilight, even though it was morning.

Suddenly, the sun cut through the darkness.

And there I was, laid in a basket inside one of the village huts, destined to be the protagonist of our story although I did not yet have a name. My family gathered around, marvelling at me, fresh to the world. The village astrologer was also present, proclaiming that I had been born under the sign of Capricorn, on the very same day as the Christian prophet.

'Look!' cried one of my brothers.

'What?'

'There, above the baby!'

Everyone looked up and saw a rainbow that had formed in the beam of light that fell through the little window.

The astrologer knew what it meant.
'He will work with colour when he grows up.'

It did not take long for the rumours to spread around the village. A rainbow child, said one. A great soul, a Mahatma, is born, said another.

When I was only one week old a cobra strayed into the hut where I was sleeping, oblivious to the impending danger. It rose above my cot and flared its muscly hood. My mother saw it and assumed it had already bitten me. She ran to me just as the snake slithered away outside. But I was fine. Indeed, I was lying there quietly, my dark eyes gazing out into the void. A miracle!

The village snake charmer told my parents that the cobra had extended its hood to protect me from raindrops dripping through the ceiling directly above my cot. The rain had been hammering at our roof for the past few days and it was now leaking. Cobras are considered holy and this was a sign from the divine. The astrologer nodded as the snake charmer spoke.

Yes, indeed. I was no ordinary baby.

The astrologer returned to tell my fortune. He took a sharpened stick and scratched my future on a palm leaf. 'He will marry a girl from far, far away, from outside the village, the district, the province, the state and even the country,' it began.

'You needn't go looking for her, she will come to you,' he whispered to me alone, looking straight into my eyes.

At first, my father could not make out the rest of the words. The astrologer held an oil lamp underneath a candlestick smeared with butter and let the soot that formed fall into the grooves scratched in the porous leaf. The text appeared before my parents' eyes. He did not need to read it out loud, my father could see the curly Oriya script for himself and read it to my mother: 'His future

2

wife will be musical, own a jungle and be born under the sign of Taurus.'

I have lived with the prophecy on the palm leaf and the stories of the rainbow and the cobra ever since I learned to understand what the adults were saying. Everyone was sure my future had been set.

I was not the only one to have my future told. The fates of all children are written in the stars the moment they are born. That is what my parents believed, and so did I, growing up.

And in some ways, I still do.

His full name is Jagat Ananda Pradyumna Kumar Mahanandia.

A joyful name. Jagat Ananda means universal happiness, and Mahanandia means optimism. But this is not his full name; this is just the short version. Including all the titles passed down from grandparents, tribe and caste, it runs to 373 letters.

But who can keep track of 373 letters? His friends settled instead on two. P (for Pradyumna) and K (for Kumar). PK.

PK's family never used any of his given names when they called out after the little boy as he ran through the village or climbed up high in the mango trees. His father used *Poa*, meaning little boy, his paternal grandparents always said *Nati*, grandson, and his mother chose *Suna Poa*, golden boy, because his skin was just a shade lighter than that of his siblings.

His first memories of the village by the river on the edge of the jungle were from after he had turned three. Or maybe he was four. Or still only two. Age was not so important. No one cared about birthdays. If you asked the villagers how old they were, their answers would vary and were never precise. Around ten, forty-something, nearly seventy, or merely young, middle-aged, very old.

However old he was, PK remembers standing inside a house with thick walls made of mud and a roof of yellowed grass. The picture comes into focus. Fields of corn with their dusty tips rustling in the evening breeze and clumps of trees with their plump leaves set alight by flowers in the winter and heavy with syrupy fruit in the spring. A stream flowed through the village and into a large river, behind which a solid wall of foliage and branches rose up from the ground. It was the beginning of the jungle, from

4

which came the occasional trumpeting of an elephant or the growl of a leopard or tiger. Wild animal tracks could often be spotted in the mud, along with piles of elephant dung or the imprint of a tiger's paw, accompanied by the buzz of swirling insects and the singing of birds.

PK's horizon was the edge of the jungle, but his universe extended beyond it and into the woods. The village and the jungle. There was nothing else. The forest was endless, mysterious, secret, but also familiar and safe. It was an adventure and yet also a certainty, a comfort. The city was somewhere he had heard about but had never seen for himself.

He lived in the hut with his mother, father and two older brothers. And his father's parents, of course. That was how most families lived; tradition dictated that the oldest son stayed with his parents, even after he had married and started his own family. Shridhar, PK's father, held fast to those traditions.

PK did not often see his father. He worked as the postmaster in Athmallik, the nearest town, which had markets, teashops, a police station and a jail. As the twenty-kilometre journey was too far to cycle every day, his father had a room with a bed at the post office where he slept during the week. Every Saturday night he would make the journey home with PK's two older brothers, who lived in the town's boarding school.

PK felt like an only child. During the week his mother devoted all her attention to him. Most days it was just the two of them and his grandparents in the house in the village on the edge of the forest.

Sunlight flooded the village, breaking through the thick canopy that often kept the forest floor in relative darkness. Most of the houses were built in the same style: round or rectangular huts of brown, dried mud, greying palm leaf roofs and bamboo enclosures for the cows and goats.

Beside them, vegetable patches had been cut into the soil and stacks of hay were piled up to be used for feed. There were some brick houses scattered around the village, built for the untouchables by the British in an act of mercy. But monsoon rains had destroyed these houses before anyone had been able to move in and now they stood empty, their ceilings collapsed. Aside from this, PK's world contained only a primary school and another building where the village council meetings were held.

PK's mother used to say that they lived in India's largest forest and that Kondpoda was its most ancient village. It was home, she said, to both the living and the dead. The sandy banks of the river were used as a cremation site, where the souls of the departed gathered at night to sing and dance. A whirlpool in the river had taken two women in recent years, both newlywed and pregnant. She had seen their bodies laid out on the beach, their foreheads embellished with dazzling red dots, shining symbols of their pure, unblemished lives. Their eyes were open wide as if searching for something, their mouths gaping as though they had screamed for help in their final moments. In reality, she told him, it was because that was how their souls had left their bodies; they had merely forgotten to close the door behind them.

At night his mother lay beside him on the straw mat, whispering stories of souls, gods, goddesses and black magic. She jangled her jewellery to create ghoulish sound effects. PK shuddered and held his breath, his heart pounding. He listened as the ghosts edged closer in the darkness, gasping, panting. But then came the warmth of his mother's body. She sensed that she scared him and pulled him close. He had gone from the laughter of the afternoon spent playing in the forest, to the bedtime horror of the valley of death and into the safety of his mother's embrace. Comforted by that feeling, he fell asleep.

His mother was not scared of the dead. She believed the best way to keep malicious spirits at bay was to show confidence, which she considered herself to possess. Only self-doubt would put you within reach of death's grip.

'As long as you are brave, no one can hurt you, not even the dead,' she would say.

Before PK started school he had no idea what a 'caste' was. No one had told him that people were divided into four main *varna*, and then into thousands of subcastes within them. He had never heard of the ancient *Rigveda* verses, thousands of years old, in which the four castes were described. He knew nothing of the mythical, primeval cosmic being Purusha, who was himself divided into four. He did not know that the Brahmins, the priests, came from Purusha's mouth. That the Kshatriya, the warriors, came from his arms, the Vaishya, the merchants, craftsmen and farmers, from his thighs, and the Shudra, the workers and servants, from his feet.

Nor had he heard of the Indo-Aryans who had come riding south from the plains of Central Asia three and a half thousand years ago and had taught the people of the Indian subcontinent's forests how to grow crops before themselves becoming priests, soldiers and administrators, assuming their position in the upper castes. He had not been told that the darker-skinned indigenous forest people ended up being consigned to the lowest groups to work as farmers, craftsmen and servants, like PK's father's family, or else lived as hunters among the trees and were known as tribal people, like his relatives on his mother's side.

By the time he reached adulthood PK had come to the conclusion that the caste system was no stranger than the feudal and subsequent class systems of Europe.

'It's not that hard,' he would say, when Westerners said they could not understand the Indian divisions.

'Okay, maybe it's a little more complicated,' he sometimes admitted.

And so he would explain that Indians were born into one of the *jati* – meaning birth – a group whose categorization functioned much like the European guild system. Jati were the subgroups of the four varna, the Sanskrit word for colour. These were the four main castes as laid out in the ancient texts of Hinduism.

'So there are only four varna but millions of jati,' PK would add.

'Millions of jati! How on earth do you keep track of them all?' the Westerners would ask. And when PK replied that they could not, no Indian could, his friends would give up and the conversation would turn to another topic.

Unless pressed, PK preferred not to tell his friends that his own family did not belong to any of the four varna and instead had no caste, that they were untouchables. Historically the designation 'untouchable' came about because they were engaged in occupations that were considered to be unclean and polluting. It was not exactly something he was proud of. And yet had he not been an untouchable, his life would have turned out very differently indeed.

The Father of the Nation, Mahatma Gandhi, had wanted to raise the status of the untouchables and so called them *Harijan*, or 'God's children'. It sounded beautiful, PK thought, but in fact this word described someone who had no proper father. Gandhi wanted to give them a pleasing name, PK supposed, a name to improve their situation in life. But somehow the label was still offensive, a rejection of the legitimacy of his flesh and blood, and one PK would disdain as an adult. After the British had left, the Indian authorities classed untouchables officially as 'Scheduled Castes', giving them cheaper train tickets and quotas to make it easier for them to attend university and be elected for public office. These well-meaning gestures of benevolence were supposedly designed to improve their lowly lot in life.

Anti-discrimination laws were drafted to combat the injustices, but laws are useless if left unenforced. Ancient prejudices are embedded in people's minds like layers of bedrock.

PK has since come to realise that change must come from within – from the heart.

In a country many thousands of miles away, Lotta had longed to visit India ever since she was twelve. She still remembers that first taste of the East, even now, when her class was shown a film about the Ganges. She watched as the sun rose over the river, accompanied by the whirr of the projector. She can recall perfectly the clang of the sitar emerging from the loudspeakers, the ringing of the temple bells and the splashing of the pilgrims as they descended the steps into the water until submerged to their waists.

This black and white film was her first introduction to India. It affected her more than anything else she was taught at school. They were asked to write essays about it; hers was a long and emotional text.

I will go there one day, Lotta said to herself.

She wanted to become an archaeologist. She loved to dig in the soil, looking for things. She dreamed of sensational discoveries, untangling the twisted yarn of history into neat threads. She chose to draw a large picture of the pyramids in class and read about the British Egyptologist Howard Carter and his discovery of Tutankhamun's tomb. The curse of the pharaohs fascinated her, excitement building in her stomach as she read about the mysterious deaths of twenty of his excavation team. Lotta wanted to spend her life solving puzzles just like these.

During her teenage years a fascination with outer space began to take over. She borrowed books about UFOs from the library and travelled to Gothenburg to listen to lectures about life on other planets. She subscribed to a specialist magazine and read every issue with feverish delight, convinced as she was that humans could not possibly be alone in the universe.

Most of all, she was interested in a life different from the one she was living. She used to fantasize about being born in the sixteenth century and living with her family in a hut in the woods. No modern luxuries or fancy gadgets. Everything stripped bare, simple, close to nature.

The only person who really understood little PK was his mother. Her name was Kalabati. She had dark blue tattoos on her face, a golden heart in her nose and moons in her ears. All that remains of her now is a brass ceremonial candlestick in the shape of an elephant. It was her favourite candlestick. PK thinks of her every time he looks at it, sitting on the mantelpiece in the yellow house in the woods.

It was Kalabati who painted the traditional magic figures on the walls of the village houses before every major festival. She had an artistic eye and was good with a brush. Her skills were in demand across all castes, including the high-caste Brahmins. As the holy days approached she rose early, washed the mud walls of the family house with cow dung and began to decorate them. Once she had completed their own home she moved on to the neighbours' houses. The day before the festivities were due to begin she worked from dawn until dusk, painting figures with spindly limbs alongside vines and flowers with slender leaves. She made the white pigment herself with rice flour and water. When she was finished, the village houses sparkled in the first pale yellow rays of morning light. These were Kalabati's great masterpieces.

PK watched his mother paint and wondered why she never worked on paper.

Kalabati was born into the Khutia Kondh tribe.

'Ordinary tribespeople like us are the descendants of the dark-skinned forest people who have lived on this land for as long as we have known, or who came here, at the very least, thousands of years before the plains people moved in and cut down the trees and began growing wheat and rice,' she told PK. 'War and disease followed them. It was the people of the plains who divided us into the worthy and the worthless. Before the Hindus came, we didn't make distinctions between people. Nobody in the forest was superior to anyone else.'

Ma was the only person who felt real to PK; the rest of his family were like strangers. An odd feeling bubbled in his stomach when his father and two older brothers rode into the village at the weekend. They only ever spent Sundays at home. Every Saturday evening his father propped his bicycle against the wall and reached to pick him up, but PK was afraid of him and cried every time.

'Don't cry – look, your father has brought sweets for you,' Kalabati would say.

He would fall silent, sniffle and then take one of the crispy sugared *burfi*, moist *gulab jamun* or chewy English toffees from his father's hand, before crawling up into his mother's lap.

Every morning Kalabati bathed PK in the Kondpoda stream. They went to the water's edge, where the fragrance of the surrounding wild flowers mingled with that of the round patties of cow dung that had been laid out to dry. His mother warned him not to swim out too far. She scrubbed his back with a fold of her sari and rubbed him with coconut oil so that he gleamed in the sunshine. He would climb up onto a stone polished smooth by the rushing water and dive into the river, before climbing back up again. He could go on like this forever. He was never cold and he never got sick, because he was protected by a layer of grease so thick that the water slid off him in pearls, keeping him warm until the sun rose high in the sky.

At the start of every summer the rivers were all but dry, awaiting the monsoon rains. The new Hirakud Dam, built a few days' canoe journey further upstream, had stripped the Mahanadi River of its wilder rapids. By June, only the smallest trickle remained in the centre of the channel. This lack of water had become a scourge on the village. It would have been one thing if they had received electricity as compensation, but the power produced in the plant was directed elsewhere. When dusk fell they turned to the crackling fires and the flames of oil lamps. Kalabati and the other women of the village took to digging makeshift wells in the large sandbanks; holes stretching down for metres, from which the water that seeped in from the sides was collected and carried home in dented tin buckets. One bucket balanced on the head and one in each hand.

According to the priests, untouchables made dirty everything that was pure and holy: they threw stones at PK whenever he approached the village temple. The year before he started school, PK decided to have his revenge. As the rituals began and the priests emerged carrying clay pots filled with water, he took his slingshot, scrabbled for stones around him, loaded and fired. Clonk, clonk, clonk! Water began to seep out of the cracks in the pots. The priests saw him and chased him through the village.

'We'll kill you!' they shouted.

He hid in a bank of cacti, the thorns digging into his flesh. Bleeding, he limped home to his mother. Even the plants want to hurt me, he thought.

Ma stroked his back and whispered softly of everything that was good, even though she knew that for untouchables and tribespeople like them, the world was mostly vindictive and unfair. He did not know why the Brahmins disliked him so much, nor why they kept him out of the temple. He had no explanation for the stones that were hurled at him. All he knew was, they stung.

His mother held back from telling him the truth and instead drew him the most beautiful pictures with her words. When the high-caste children touched PK by mistake,

14

they ran away and washed themselves in the river.

'Why do they do that?' he asked.

'Because they're dirty,' his mother replied. 'They need a wash! Eugh, so stinky and dirty!' she repeated until he no longer took their actions as a reflection of his own self-worth.

Kalabati had never been to school and so could neither read nor write. But she knew a lot about the world, nevertheless. Like how to make pigments, paint intricate designs and mix leaves, seeds and roots into natural remedies.

Her life was shaped by routine. Chores were always performed at the same time every day. She got up before the sun, her alarm the crowing roosters and the morning sun's position in the sky her clock face. PK lay on his straw mat and listened as she scrubbed the floor, veranda and yard with a mixture of water and cow pat. He thought it strange that she used dung for cleaning, until she explained that it was far more effective than any white chemical powder you could buy in the village shop.

After cleaning the house, Kalabati went to fertilize the family's field of corn and then bathe in the river. She returned and stood in her dark blue sari on the newly swept veranda. Her wet, curly hair glistened in the morning sun as she slowly squeezed the water out with a cotton cloth.

She sang softly as she watered the fragrant green-purple leaves of the holy basil bush. Then she went to the kitchen and dipped her index finger in a clay pot of red cinnabar powder and pressed it to the middle of her forehead. She looked at herself in the cracked mirror that hung on a hook by the stove. Leaning towards it, she painted thick black lines around her eyes with homemade kohl, a mixture of soot and ghee.

Then it was PK's turn to get up. He rolled up his straw mat and he received a dot of kohl in the middle of his forehead to protect him against evil. This was then followed by a dab of ghee, which soon melted in the sun and dribbled down his face. The butter was Kalabati's way of telling the rest of the village they were not as poor as they seemed.

'Not everyone can afford butter and milk,' she told him, 'but we can.'

Look! The Mahanandia family lets the butter run down their children's faces! At least, that was what Kalabati hoped they would think.

His body clean, hair combed, kohl and butter smeared on his forehead, PK was ready for the new day.

His mother's ancestors, the tribal people, had hunted among the trees and farmed in the glades for thousands of years. Nowadays, most of Kalabati's relatives worked making bricks by the riverside. They collected mud from the bottom of the river, shaped and fired it. PK's uncle, however, held fast to the old ways and made his living with a sling, hunting in the forest. PK received a peacock feather from him, which he tied to a string and fastened around his head while he played at creeping about the forest, pretending that he too was on the hunt.

Kalabati secretly wished for a daughter, so had let PK's hair grow and helped him tie it up in braids. PK was proud of them, and liked to tie stones to their ends. 'Look how strong my hair is!' he roared at the other children, swinging the rocks from his braids.

The other boys, who wore their hair short, were impressed. They had never seen anything like it.

He usually played naked save for some wristbands and a belt strung with white shells. All Khutia Kondh children ran around like this. The caste Hindus thought the tribal people strange; their children were covered up.

Kalabati worshipped the sun and sky, monkeys and cows, peacocks, cobras and elephants. She worshipped the liquorish scent of the tulsi bush, as well as the peepal sacred fig and the neem tree, whose antibacterial sap was used for cleaning teeth. To her, the divine had no name, but it was present in everything around them. Several times a week she went to a grove where the trees grew so close that they formed walls on all sides. Inside this secret temple hewn from nature, she gathered stones and fresh grass, laid out a small amount of butter and sprinkled red cinnabar powder over it. There she prayed to all the living things in the forest, but especially to the trees, which, along with the sun, were the most holy of all.

Just like the other tribes of India's eastern forests, the Khutia Kondh had never divided themselves into castes, nor made any distinction between chiefs and subjects. Everyone had the same right to worship the gods and communicate with the divine. But then something happened. Kalabati told PK how the people from the north-western plains came, and how they began to cultivate the valleys and riversides. They regarded the forest people as primitive and uncivilized.

'In the end, we were forced into their caste system,' his mother said sadly.

The forest people tried on occasion to revolt. The British had to send troops to restore order. But it was an uneven battle in which PK's people were uniformly defeated. When PK was in his twenties, he read that Maoist guerrilla warriors called the Naxalites had once again taken on the fight for the rights of the tribal people. Gradually, the conflict escalated and the Indian army went in with force. Blood was shed, hatred took hold, and the newspapers called the conflict a civil war. PK did not like this violent turn. He realized that many of his mother's kinsmen felt all hope had been lost when the mining companies started exploiting their sacred mountains, trees and shrubs for minerals. At first, he too thought the only solution was to fight back. But then PK's hate subsided. No man was worth so little that he deserved to die, not even an oppressor or a murderer. PK agreed with Mahatma Gandhi when he said, 'An eye for an eye makes the whole world blind.'

Athmallik had been one of India's 565 princely states during the years of the British Empire, a Lilliputian country of some forty thousand inhabitants. Not that it was ever a 'real' country: the King had been subordinate to the British and was forced, like all the others, to abdicate when the Empire retreated in 1947 to make way for a modern state apparatus and democratically elected politicians.

The founding of the kingdom of Athmallik was shrouded in mystery. The royal family claimed to be heirs to a traditional ruling clan from Jaipur in Rajasthan. One of the King's sons, named Protap Deo, left their crumbling palace in Jaipur with his brothers and travelled eastward to conquer Puri, the grand temple city by the shores of Bengal Bay. But their plan failed, and they were forced to flee up the Mahanadi River, inland towards the forests. After a few days' march upstream, Protap Deo founded his kingdom, taking over a collection of villages nestled in a clearing. He killed the local indigenous chief and installed himself on the throne.

People said that before the kings arrived, when the tribal chiefs still ruled, the god Jagannath lived in a cave hidden in the forested mountains of Athmallik. The god was represented by a wide-eyed, limbless wooden statue worshipped by the indigenous Sabar people. But one day, Hindu priests arrived along the river by boat and kidnapped Jagannath, installing him in the main temple of Puri, where he has remained ever since. The god was thus brought into the Hindu pantheon to be worshipped by millions of pilgrims from all over India. In Athmallik, Jagannath is believed to have once been adorned by what was then the largest diamond in the world, before became known as the Koh-i-Noor and joined the British royal family's collection of crown jewels via the Mughals, Persians and Sikhs.

In 1827, a British colonel named Gilbert arrived and was made director of the South-west Frontier Agency in Athmallik. The King, he discovered, was in conflict with the neighbouring Boud on the other side of the river. The King of Boud regarded the King of Athmallik as his subordinate and demanded he pay tribute, but because the rulers of Athmallik did not consider theirs a vassal kingdom, they refused to pay. The British colonel noted that, every now and then, the King of Boud made incursions into Athmallik and stole livestock and other valuables. Gilbert must have rubbed his hands in glee. A local dispute! The area could not be better placed for a takeover, perfect for the British and their policy of divide and rule.

When PK was a child, the people of Athmallik still talked about the days of princely rule. That time was doused in a shimmer of nostalgia. PK's relatives did well during that time, and his paternal grandfather had the great honour of being assigned the task of capturing wild elephants for the King and taming them for service in court. According to custom, the elephant catcher's children and grandchildren were held in high regard by the royal family.

The kings of Athmallik did not fight the British. They acceded to the demands of the imperialists for political supremacy and control of trade, and accepted gratefully the offer of protection. The British rewarded their acquiescence in 1890 by upgrading their raja, Mahendra Deo Samant, a king, to the title of Maharaja, Great King.

And yet despite their relative privilege during the time of the princes, it was under the British that PK's family was really to prosper.

When King Bibhudendra died in 1918, the heir to the throne was only fourteen years old and too young to accede, so Colonel Cobden-Ramsay took over temporarily. Ramsay was known to his subjects as the White Raja, and he governed the princely state of Athmallik for seven years. According to PK's grandfather, those were the seven best years in living memory.

'Cobden-Ramsay wasn't a racist like the other Englishmen,' his grandfather would say. 'He didn't pay attention to caste.' The British, in contrast to many Indians, cared about the common good and not just how to enrich themselves.

'Can you name one single Brahmin who treated anyone outside their own caste with even a shred of respect or dignity?' his grandfather would ask. 'Have any of them ever done anything to benefit the lower castes? No, exactly! But the British did, all the time. They acted on behalf of everyone and never discriminated against us untouchables.'

PK's family liked and respected the British. It was the first time they had known rich and powerful men who did not see them as ritually unclean. They knew India's elite hated the British. But PK's grandfather used to say that he had never met an untouchable who resented the British colonial masters.

Mahatma Gandhi said the British were racists. That might have been true, but PK's grandfather believed Gandhi never understood that the worst racism to plague Indian society was the treatment of untouchables by high-caste Hindus.

PK's grandfather, grandmother and father had all attended Victoria Vernacular School in Kaintragarh, the tiny kingdom's capital, where they learned to read and write and even speak a little English.

'Before the British came, there was of course no school for us,' Grandpa said. 'But then everyone got to go to school!' he shouted, almost triumphantly. The British did not make distinctions between the local population – high caste and low were of equal worth. 'It didn't matter which caste we belonged to. Oh, it was such a joy to get to learn. For the first time, we saw that someone outside our group wished us well.'

During Queen Victoria's birthday celebrations every year, Grandpa was allowed to raise the British flag at school while the other children sang the British national anthem. Many years later, PK's European friends found it hard to understand that his relatives could feel joy at performing such a ceremony when his country had been colonized, occupied and subordinated to a foreign power. But Athmallik had almost always been ruled by outsider kings, he explained. Hundreds of years ago, King Ashoka was conquered by Emperor Kharavela, who was succeeded by the Sultan of Bengal and then the Maratha Empire.

'The British were only one in a long line of foreign rulers,' PK said. 'But as long as the foreign kings didn't interfere in the lives of the ordinary people, the locals didn't care too much who was in charge.'

Yet British rule changed the power dynamics within the villages for the first time. They did not understand the caste system, at least not in the way the Brahmins wanted them to. The British hired untouchables to work in the post office, the civil service and on the railways. And anyone who wanted to could attend Victoria Vernacular School.

'No, the British have nothing to be ashamed of,' was Grandpa's opinion.

The kings of Athmallik had not been extravagantly rich. Not like the maharajas of Rajasthan in western India who lived in enormous palaces and kept hundreds of elephants, hung hunting trophies on their walls and filled their drawers with diamonds. And certainly not like the maharaja who owned twenty-seven Rolls-Royces or the maharaja who married his daughter off to a prince in a wedding *The Guinness Book of Records* described as the most lavish in the world. Or like the maharaja who arranged a wedding for two of his dogs, dressing 250 canine guests in gemstone-encrusted brocade outfits to receive the 'bridegroom' astride a train of decorated elephants. Such profligacy was unknown in the miniature kingdom in which PK grew up.

By the time PK was born, most of the maharajan palaces and office buildings were already abandoned and dilapidated. Liana vines had begun to wrap their strong stems around the increasingly monsoon-mouldy walls and collapsed roofs. The son of the last ruling maharaja of Athmallik left the palace when India became independent, but as the owner of a successful business, he moved instead into a stately mansion. PK and his family were always welcome there for a chat, a cup of tea and to gaze at the framed sepia photographs of the British dressed in pith helmets and Indian princes in turbans. Indeed, PK is as welcome there today as he was as a child.

Despite their status as untouchable, PK's father, grandmother and grandfather still belonged to the Hindu faithful. His father performed Hindu rituals at home, but not all untouchables did so. PK suspected that his father's beliefs were inspired by his high-caste colleagues at the post office. Shridhar put together a small altar with pictures of Lakshmi, the goddess of prosperity, Ganesh, the elephant protector, and a statuette of Vishnu, the Sustainer of the Universe, surrounded by incense and oil lamps. Every day, wrapped in sweet smells and smoke from the fire, his father prayed to the gods for a happy life for himself and his family.

As long as there were no Brahmins nearby, untouchables were able to approach the Shiva temple. But no untouchable ever dared enter the innermost rooms where the statues of the gods were enthroned. Such impudence would have thrown the Brahmins into an ungodly rage.

Local custom claimed that hurting or killing snakes brought bad luck, so they had made the village temple their home. The priests fed the snakes every day because they believed it to be Shiva's wish. PK liked that the villagers looked after the snakes. He had peered into the temple and spotted a metal cobra glinting in the darkness, its neck extended as it protected the gods just as the real cobra had done when he was a baby. The snakes were mankind's friends, PK was sure of that.

The temple was also the place you went if you were bitten by a snake. There, you would be laid on your stomach in front of the entrance and told to pray to Shiva. Sooner or later, the Auspicious One would answer and heal your wounds. PK saw it with his own eyes when his aunt had suffered a particularly fierce attack. As custom dictated, she went to the temple, lay down on the steps and prayed. Then she went home and slept. The next morning she got up and announced that she was fully recovered. It was a miracle by Shiva's own hand, everyone could see that.

Shiva's powers were not limited to snake bites. One of PK's aunts had been married for twelve years without bearing a child. She went to the temple, lay down on the steps to pray, and there she stayed for four days and four nights. She neither ate nor spoke; her devotion took all her energy. She returned home weak and tired, and had to be brought to the table to be fed rice. Nine months later, she gave birth to her first baby.

The gods did not confine themselves to the temples. A nearby clump of cacti was home to Sat Devi, the Seven Goddesses who had their origins in the beliefs of the forest people but had since come to be feared by the Hindus. The goddesses possessed great powers, people said. Bad things happened if they were not respected.

The priests performed ceremonies to appease the goddesses before the villagers went out to collect seeds for the next year's crops. But one man did not wait for the ritual to be completed, and before long, he was struck down with aches and a raging fever. The muscles in his legs atrophied, until they became as thin as twigs. He never recovered. For the rest of his life he was forced to drag himself around on crutches. That was what happened if you defied the goddesses.

An old tree grew at the eastern end of the village, where bats and nocturnal birds lived. And witches, said PK's grandmother. Every night, a conference of birds could be heard chatting in the tree, only to be drowned out by the shrill squawks of the crows, the most fervent talkers of all. But PK thought that these noises were actually the desperate cries of people who had been cursed by the witches and damned to spend this life in bird form.

A large wooden cart was usually parked on the outskirts of the village. During the summer festivities it was used to parade the black, white and yellow gods: Jagannath, Lord of the Universe, his brother Balarama and sister Subhadra. They were gods of the forest people, ones his mother's family had worshipped since ancient times even though the Hindus had made them their own. Jagannath became a revelation of Vishnu, while the Buddhists saw him as an incarnation of the Buddha.

In autumn, festival season came again. This was when Durga, Shiva's wife, was honoured. The priests sacrificed goats on a hill outside the village, staining the soil dark with their blood. The Brahmins said that blood gave Durga power to fight the demons that threatened the divine order.

The Hindus have so many gods, PK used to think. He never understood how they all fitted together. But he felt their presence and ignored the contradictions. As an adult, he realized that his mother and father were not allowed to participate fully in the festivals. They could join the processions, but were forbidden to touch the statues or the wooden cart in which the gods travelled. They could pray, but not next to the upper castes or in the temple. They were permitted to perform the rituals, but preferably in the background so that the Brahmins did not see them. If the priests had been free to decide, they would have made the untouchables stay at home, away from everything that was pure and holy.

A great deal of Indian entertainment focused on relationships between mothers and daughters-in-law, the core conflict at the heart of the Indian family and thus the subject of many soap operas and Bollywood films. This was perhaps only natural when multiple generations lived together under one roof. Men may be the masters of the mountainside, but women reign over the hearth. To this day, mothers-in-law maintain a firm grip over the domestic realm, while daughters-in-law bring habits inherited from their own mothers. How should the chapatis be rolled, the dal boiled, the corn harvested and the children raised?

PK was three years old and too young to notice what was going on in his own family, but his older brothers later told him about the time their mother fell out with Grandma.

Kalabati had given birth to her fourth child three months earlier, a girl named Pramodini. But her mother-in-law was on the attack.

'That beloved wife of yours is a witch,' she told Shridhar.

And then she turned to Kalabati. 'You can't stay here. You bring trouble on us all.'

Kalabati's eyes darkened, but she did not reply. What good would it do to protest? It was understood by all that Grandma made the decisions. The house belonged to her and her husband. PK's mother was the outsider who had moved in. The only person in a position to defend her was Shridhar, but he said nothing. He swallowed the anger, vexation and shame. He showed no emotion, no displeasure at his mother's behaviour.

Silence descended on the home. That Monday, Shridhar left for the city without comment and Kalabati went about her chores. But after a week had passed and Shridhar was about to return for the weekend, Kalabati turned to her mother-in-law. Without letting even one tear run down her cheeks, she announced that she would be moving back to her parents.

'With the two youngest.'

Grandma put her foot down. 'Take the girl, she's just a baby, but the boy stays with me.'

Kalabati accepted without a word.

PK stood on the veranda with his arms crossed and his cheeks wet with crying as his mother took her possessions in one arm, his little sister in the other, and, weighed down by a heavy frown, walked out of the house and down the path. She turned several times to look at him; he waved and she waved back. To this day, he can still see her disappearing behind the sugar cane and feel how his world suddenly became quiet and empty.

His mother and little sister were gone. As his Bapa Shridhar lived six days a week in the city, PK was alone with his grandmother and grandfather.

He cried for days, weeks, maybe even months. Tears showered his cheeks as the monsoon clouds expelled sheets of rain that turned the dirt roads scarlet and made the straw ceilings smell of damp and mould. Everything was a wet haze of loss. Once he had cried out all his tears, he fell silent. He stopped talking, laughing, even smiling. He spent days with the same pinched face. He refused to let a word pass his lips. Most of his waking time was spent sitting by himself in a corner, staring into space. He refused food, but soon he did not have the strength to fight when Grandma forced him to eat. The rice and lentils had no flavour any more. Food was just texture in his mouth.

Then, one Sunday, a man came riding up on a bicycle. He had a message from Kalabati's family; she had been taken ill. She no longer did her chores, the messenger said. She just sat and cried. Shridhar received the news and, without letting anyone know what he was thinking, walked quietly out into the back garden, fetched his mother, who was digging in the soil, and led her off to the cornfield.

'We can't go on like this!' he cried, finally releasing months of imprisoned anger.

His mother made no reply.

'You are driving my wife insane!' he continued.

Still she said nothing.

What could she say? She was too proud to admit that she had made a mistake. And deep down, she probably thought she was in the right. She was a stubborn woman. Unyielding. She represented reason and logic in the face of a world gone mad.

When PK's Bapa returned the following Saturday, he sat PK down and told him that he had purchased a piece of land near the post office in the town of Athmallik.

'We are going to move there, to our new house,' he said.

'Who's we?'

'Us. Just us.'

'We're going to live there by ourselves?' PK asked. He had never heard of anyone who did not live with their grandparents.

'Yes, it will be our house. Just ours,' Shridhar confirmed.

The rain polished the sugar cane and churned the red soil into mud, so that cows and people squelched and bicycle wheels scored deep combat-zone furrows in the muck. Black clouds gathered above and the landscape was enveloped in semi-darkness, cheating the villagers of precious daylight hours.

Bapa lifted PK up onto the cart, which was tied behind two glossy oxen. It had a roof of plaited bamboo, and a couple of burnt clay pots filled with milk from Grandma and Grandpa's cow had been loaded onto the back. The driver belted the animals with his whip and the wheels started to roll, settling into a leisurely rhythmic creak as they made their way through the village.

Bapa walked behind with Grandma and Grandpa, talking, while PK sat close to his mother, who had placed his little sister in her lap. He could not hear what his father was saying, but he hoped that he was explaining why they could not stay, that they were moving to make his mother happy again.

After a few short minutes, the cart stopped by the spirit tree outside the temple on the outskirts of the village. PK looked back and saw his father kneeling down before Grandma, his forehead lowered to the ground. He was touching her feet with his fingertips.

It started to rain again, the plump drops saturating Grandma's grey hair and yellow sari. But no tears ran down her cheeks. The ox cart continued to roll along the narrow earthen road between the fields. PK looked around again as the temple and the cornfields receded and then disappeared completely in the lingering fog.

Grandma dissolved away with the rest of the village, a quivering yellow dot in the grey, before becoming one with the monsoon and the nightfall.

He laid his head on his mother's lap. She covered his naked body with a piece of thin, soft cotton.

The cart rocked along the road, winding through woods, past flooded rice fields and across narrow wooden bridges that hovered above hurried streams and rivers. The rain clouds blocked out any residual light from the stars or the moon. PK looked out into the darkness and saw nothing. But his ears were attuned to the creaking of the wheels and to the familiar sounds of the forest: croaking frogs, singing grasshoppers and screaming foxes. He felt the warmth of his mother's soft thighs and was calmed by the rhythm of her breathing.

He awoke as his mother stroked his forehead to announce their arrival. Paralysed by fatigue, PK was helped down from the cart. He stared into the darkness, but there was nothing to see. Where was their new house?

Father lit an oil lamp and their new home emerged from the shadows. Long grass tickled his legs.

'Where are we?' he asked.

'Liptinga Sahi,' replied his mother. 'Close to Athmallik, near where your father works and your brothers go to school.'

Father disappeared to get some food from the kitchens of the private school. He soon returned with metal lunchboxes filled to the brim. They sat on the floor of their new home and ate their first meal in their new village, far, far away from Grandma and Grandpa. Life had suddenly taken on a new colour, thought PK, as he watched the insects fly into the white glow of the gas lamp. Even the dal had been made with different spices, he noted in amazement. Taste had returned. The cloud of grief that had hung over the family began to fade into the past.

Nobody would ever be able to separate him from his mother again.

The new house sat alone, separate from the others. But PK frequently heard the sound of children shouting and laughing.

'They are our people,' his mother said, patting him on the head.

'Our people?'

'They belong to the same caste as us.'

It was the first time he had heard the word, even if he had experienced its vicious sting back in the old village. He understood, however, that it meant the children would not mind playing with him. That they belonged together.

'Caste?' he repeated.

'Yes, they are Pan, just like your father.'

'What about you, Ma?' asked PK.

'I'm Kondh. Khutia Kondh.'

He was learning so much in this new place.

A path cut through the cornfields, passed their house and the others further beyond, and on towards a crumbling, yellow concrete building with a small hatch window secured by thick metal bars. It was along this trail that the long stream of village men stumbled to get their hooch. They shouted to the man inside and out came large bottles of beer and smaller bottles of spirits wrapped in brown paper bags. They turned up in the early morning until the sun disappeared for the night, singing and wailing, the whites of their eyes shot through with blood. This was PK's first encounter with alcohol. He had never seen a drunk before.

Another narrow road went from the house down to a large reservoir. He liked following the paths and exploring where they led. Every day he ventured just a little bit further than the last. But he was always careful to avoid the hooch shop because the men, stinking of spirits, shouted after him, grabbed him and slurred so badly he could not understand what they were saying.

At his grandparents' house they had bathed in the river. In Liptinga Sahi they washed in the reservoir, which was covered in lotus flowers and teaming with fish. Many of the villagers took their morning bath here, along with birds and bears looking for breakfast. His mother would dig damp clay from the wooded embankment close to the water's edge and take it home in a basket. She used the mud to wash her hair and clean the plates, pots and pans.

'Gravel and clay mixed together work better than soap and water,' Kalabati said. She made a virtue out of buying as little as possible from the shop, so that she could save their money for more important things.

By the time the first monsoon clouds had passed overhead and the autumn sun was high in the sky, PK had begun to feel at home. It almost felt as if they had never lived anywhere else. He adapted quickly; indeed, he always had.

If you don't adapt, you drown, he came to realize many years later.

One day, his mother took him on a walk to the two largest trees on the outskirts of the village. They were home to eagles and vultures. Under the trees men worked skinning dead cows, preparing the hides to sell to the shoemaker to make into shoes and bags.

'They,' she said, pointing to the men, 'are our people.'

'Do we know them?' he asked.

'No, they belong to the same caste as us.'

But that was not entirely true. The men who took care of the animal carcasses came from a group of families that belonged to the Ghasiara caste. They lived in the forest, beyond the cornfields. But they were also untouchables, which was what his mother meant. The Ghasis lived in terrible conditions. The Brahmins considered them even dirtier than the Pan because not only did they work with dead animals, but they handled the carcasses of cows. God forbid. Even their shadows were dirty. The merest sight of them was considered a bad omen.

But as darkness fell, the Ghasi women were no longer untouchable, that much Kalabati knew. At night-time the men from the surrounding villages came, men who were ritually clean and distinguished, to buy sex from the women. Even Brahmins, who spat on them during the hours of daylight, were drawn to their tents at night.

Kalabati did not tell her son about this. She wanted to protect him from the cruel reality of life for the untouchables for as long as possible.

PK stood in the cornfield and watched the Ghasi men drag a dead cow towards the village spirit tree. Their second monsoon in the new house was upon them. He watched as they laid the heavy body out on the ground and began separating the skin from the flesh and the flesh from the bones. Flies swarmed around the mounds of meat and vultures circled ever lower. Finally, the birds shot down from the sky like arrows. But rather than tear into their dinner, they waited, like stone statues, patience winning out over greed. It looked to PK as if the vultures had been possessed by the gods, or at least, they did not act like predators. He could not understand why they were not eating. He looked up. Two more birds were flying above. Then, suddenly, they too swept down with such force that their wings whipped the air into cyclones.

PK dreamed of being able to do the same. He took off down the sloping path that meandered towards their house, howling like a vulture, his arms stretched out like wings.

'Ma, if I sat on the back of one of those vultures, would I be able to fly too?' he asked when they were home.

But instantly, his dreams of flying were dispelled.

'Be careful of vultures!' his mother replied quickly. 'They will peck your eyes out and turn you blind!'

'Why did they wait before eating?'

'Vultures,' she said, 'are just like people. They have kings and queens, sons and daughters and live in families too. When a cow dies the vultures tell their king and queen where the body is located. They daren't eat before the king and queen. That's why they wait so patiently like that.'

Then she continued: 'The king and queen are the most beautiful of all the vultures. Look closely next time: their feathers shimmer like gold in the sun.'

She put her hand on his forehead.

'Their world is not so different from ours.'

PK's maternal grandmother lived alone in a small village a few kilometres further into the jungle. Her house was even humbler, with walls made of bamboo and mud and a thatched roof that often collapsed during the monsoon rains. The garden had been overtaken by tall maize plants, which attracted wild animals when the corn was ripe. Regulars included the bear, with his long, black coat, and the fox. When Grandma tired of seeing her precious maize crop being taken, she built a scarecrow out of straw and placed it high up in a clump of bamboo. She hung a brass bell that tinkled in the breeze from one of its arms. This kept most of the animals away. But not all of them.

PK and his little sister Pramodini were visiting their grandma one evening when a family of *hathi* came to visit. The children were already asleep when the walls around them began to shake. Two adult elephants and their baby were trampling the vegetation and chewing on the bright yellow corncobs. But Grandma was not scared. She went out on the veranda with a bundle of dry grass, set it alight and started waving the flames at them. Unfortunately, the elephants were not scared either. The papa elephant snorted, scuffed the ground with his hind foot and charged straight at Grandma. She threw the torch and ran back to the hut, slamming the wooden door behind her and locking it.

The elephant threw his weight against the fragile building, cracking the mud and bamboo walls. Grandma woke the grandchildren, told PK to get out of the way and, with little Pramodini on her hip, began banging at the opposite wall with her one free fist, managing to beat a hole in it large enough to escape through. She nudged PK outside and they ran through the thorny undergrowth and cacti. PK remembers feeling nothing as the thorns ripped through his skin. Blood gushed down his legs, but he was numb. Was he awake, or still asleep and dreaming?

Finally they stopped, exhausted. PK had no idea how far they had run. Their escape was quick but it felt infinitely long. Soaked in blood and sweat, they collapsed against a tree trunk and waited for the sun to rise. The night air was filled with the buzz and chirp of mosquitoes, grasshoppers and crickets.

'What if the elephants are angry with us? What if they come after us and trample us to death?'

But luckily they never did, and Grandma, PK and Pramodini were sore but safe.

In this northern country no wild elephants roamed. Instead, mosquitoes buzzed in the reeds that edged the wooded lakes of Borås. Willow warblers serenaded each other, while moose and deer grazed among the fir trees in the hundred-year-old forests. Rainwater glistened in the tracks left by large forest machinery. Grey smoke rose from the chimneys of the red summer cottages that dotted the glades.

Lotta's family were regular church-goers. Lotta's mother grew up fearing purgatory, haunted by the priest's descriptions of the eternal punishment that awaited sinners in the next life. Her father joined them at the weekly service even though he was not himself a believer. Lotta was never sure what he thought about religion and the Church; he rarely expressed his opinions about anything. He was a hard man to get to know. There were moments when she thought she might understand him, especially when they sat side-by-side in silence. Somehow, she felt a deep connection to him despite the lack of conversation.

When Lotta was eight, one of her aunts fell ill while pregnant. The family prayed to God, but her aunt's condition worsened. Both aunt and baby died, and the faith Lotta had once felt was subsumed by anger and disappointment.

She was confirmed into the Swedish Church, but not because she had faith. No, she did it mostly because that was what everyone did. She was easily influenced by parents and friends. It was hard to be different, to do her own thing. People turned against those who broke the norm, stuck out too much. Lotta had no strong beliefs in any case; she found it difficult to attach too much weight to any one idea. There was a hint of truth in most things people said and she took little interest in politics. How could one put one's faith in a party, or an ideology, one hundred per cent? To do so meant that everyone else had to be completely wrong. No, party politics was not for her.

Sometimes she found herself humming a song that she had first learned at the age of three. Its message: a light shone over all of humanity, despite its vanity, its ambition and its pettiness.

That light exists inside me too, thought Lotta. But it was not God, it was something else:

> Clouds come, clouds go
> Sometimes the heart goes cold
> But up above us, in the sky
> A wishing star behold.

Instead, in her teens, her imagination turned eastwards. She read the *Upanishads* and continued with the *Vedas* and the Buddha's sermons. There were similarities between the ancient Hindu texts and the Bible's Sermon on the Mount, she observed. But there was something wrong in the way Christianity expressed its teaching. It excluded more than it embraced. Christians seemed more interested in drawing boundaries between people. Everyone, whether they were believers or not, was driven by the same vital energy. The heart beats for the same reason in all of us, no matter your beliefs, she thought. All atoms in the universe belong together. Everything is connected.

The Asian philosophies made a strong impression on her, especially the idea that all humans and animals dissolve after their death and come alive again in other living things. Yes, that's it, she thought. If you want to know the past, look at the present. If you want to know the future, look again at the present, as the Buddha said.

Life is recycled and recreated again and again. We have all been soil and water and it is to soil and water we will return, thought the teenaged Lotta.

When the Pan men shot a sambar deer, PK's grandfather would be invited to sample the meat. Around festival time, villagers came with auspicious gifts of tiger skins and bird feathers. Grandpa's elevated social standing rubbed off on PK, and among the untouchable children he was king. He was proud of his grandfather and liked to imitate him. With a bow and arrow Grandpa had given him as a present, he led groups of friends on expeditions into the jungle, naked as usual save for a peacock feather and a belt and bracelet shaped like snakes. They crept along paths and pretended to hunt tiger and deer. They howled with excitement at every squirrel that scampered up a nearby tree or eagle that circled above the forest canopy.

They pretended that PK was their chief while the other children took turns acting as his spiritual adviser. This boy would pick fruit for PK and present it to him with a bow. Then they ran down to the river to fish or ventured into the woods to strike at beehives hanging high up in the branches.

The beehives were PK's domain. He climbed up with a bundle of dry grass, set fire to it and held it underneath to smoke out the bees. He clasped a stick in his mouth, which he used to jab at the hive to scare away any bees still brave enough to remain inside. Sometimes the bees launched their own counterattack. But no matter how badly he was stung, PK refused to retreat without having first tasted the sweet nectar inside. With one hand wrapped around the tree trunk, he greedily sucked on his stick as the honey ran down his cheeks and dribbled onto his chest. Then he let some drip down to the others, waiting below, their mouths gaping as the sweet, sticky drops fell from the sky.

* * *

PK was also becoming the village artist. He collected big, smooth stones along the road out of the village, and drew on them in charcoal. Sunrises, sunsets and wooded mountains.

PK's skills advanced quickly. He took the neighbouring children to a large, flat rock near the river, told them to close their eyes, and then declared that with his magical powers he could lure a tiger and make it stand before them. They were sceptical, but obeyed. He started working. There, on the stone, he drew a tiger with its mouth wide open in a roar. 'Look!' he cried. The other children stared in astonishment. Were they frightened? Had he convinced them? Maybe it was just wishful thinking. Then they laughed in delight.

At least I can make people happy with my drawing, he thought.

He expanded his repertoire and honed his technique. He painted in every spare moment he had, before and after class, and all of Sunday. He found stones in a variety of colours, not just beige and grey. He discovered how to use leaves and flowers to produce pigments other than black. He learned to make plates out of clay from the river and then paint designs on them, which he brushed with a layer of egg yolk to make them fast. He also worked on paper and favoured jungle motifs such as leaves, flowers and trees.

Every stone within a hundred metres of their house was transformed into a work of art. Here was his gallery. And inside, a row of decorated plates stood proud on a shelf.

These games in the woods are among PK's most treasured childhood memories. The forest spoke to him and his desire for adventure. It was full of secrets and surprises that he knew would only reveal themselves gradually. The rest was destined to remain mysterious and unknowable. He has held onto this feeling to the present day. It is enough to comprehend only a small part of life. He is content knowing that there is much he will never understand.

PK's father pedalled energetically, a whistle dancing from his lips. He was in a good mood. The road wove between cornfields, mango groves and clusters of mud houses. His white shirt beat in the wind as he swerved potholes, stones and twigs. PK was just as happy. He sat on the carrier, his father's shirt a sail spread out before him. They were on the way to town, away from the safety of their people, but he felt brave and adventurous, and relished the feeling of uncertainty.

Finally, he was starting school.

The teacher of his new primary school in Athmallik had promised Shridhar that his son would be allowed to join the class even though the semester had begun a month before. Perhaps his mother and father had delayed the decision, fearful about how PK would be treated. In light of their own bitter experiences, no doubt.

The school was made up of a row of ochre classrooms built in mud, sharing a long veranda that faced a sandy schoolyard. The outer boundary was marked by a dense wall of greenery made from bamboo sticks and vines.

PK peered into the classroom. There sat his new teacher, his belly large and round. The teacher turned to look at him.

'Just like Ganesh,' the old man chuckled as he patted himself on the stomach.

Then he turned back to the other students, and pointed to the letters written on the blackboard. The children sang back the words in unison.

So many children, so many new friends.

The teacher stopped and gestured to his place. But his finger was not pointing in the direction of the other children, but to the veranda outside.

'There,' he said. 'You sit there, Pradyumna Kumar Mahanandia!'

PK sat cross-legged on the sandy floor outside. He felt confused and disappointed. Why am I sitting on my own out here? But his father took no notice. What was it that he knew that PK did not? He pressed PK's hand, said goodbye, and walked over to his bike leaning against the bamboo fence.

PK was alone with all these unfamiliar people. Did they want to be his friend? He was no longer so sure. The excitement of the ride had now dissipated. Why was the teacher angry with him? Why was he not allowed to sit on the floor inside the classroom, with all the others?

The teacher soon came out to the veranda to help him with the writing exercise. He spread a thin layer of sand over PK's wooden board and showed him how to draw the letters with his forefinger in the grains. PK noticed that the teacher avoided touching him. He sat close, but was careful not to make contact. Why was he acting like this?

From the veranda, PK could see into the classroom as the teacher turned and began to write the letter 'ma' on the blackboard in Oriya. 'Repeat,' he instructed.

'Ma, ma, ma, ma, ma,' chanted PK and the rest of the class.

The teacher rang a brass bell to announce time for play. The students rushed out into the yard, so PK stood up to follow them.

'Where are you going?' cried the teacher.

The question rendered PK mute. Was it not obvious?

'You're not to play with them!' continued the teacher.

PK adapted surprisingly quickly. On the first day of school, he spent break time by himself in a corner of the playground, fighting back the tears. On the second day, he discovered a pond behind the school where he could play on his own. Within a week, he found himself longing for those solitary moments. He did not understand why it had to be like this. He gazed at his reflection in the water. He searched the rippled image for the features, the colour perhaps, that made him different from the others. Maybe his nose was too flat, his complexion too dark, his hair too curly? Sometimes he thought he looked more like the forest creatures that played on the dark surface of the water. Other times he concluded that, in fact, he looked just like all the other children.

After a week, he finally asked his mother what he should have asked the first evening, but was too confused to formulate into words.

'Why do I have to sit outside the classroom?'

His mother was squatting by the fire in the kitchen, grilling corn on the cob and baking chapatis. She looked at him.

'Why am I not allowed to play with the others?' he continued.

'We are jungle people,' she said at last.

He looked at her and felt even more confused. What did she mean?

'Once upon a time, our people lived deep in the woods. We probably should have stayed there and led our lives among the trees and not moved to the village to live with people from the plains.'

She picked him up and sat him on her lap.

'We are not allowed in the temple, because it makes the priests angry. You already noticed that. We are not allowed to draw water from the same well as the others. That's why I go to the river or the reservoir and not the common well. But there's nothing we can do about it. We just have to accept it.'

'Why?' he asked.

'Because we are untouchable, because we have been born to a lower caste... or... to no caste at all.'

She caught his eye.

'It will all work out, you'll see, only if you focus on the truth…' She wiped her tears. '… And as long as you are honest with yourself and other people.'

That evening, he lay on his straw mat and pondered what his mother had told him. The whooshing of bats and howling of dogs were the accompaniment to his thoughts. Ma gathered sticks for the fire and rattled stainless steel bowls. These were his safe sounds, the ones he fell asleep to every night. But somehow he could not quiet his mind. What did caste mean? And untouchable? He sensed that it explained his teacher's strange behaviour, but where did it come from? Why was everyone so obsessed with it?

PK's class had been assigned a piece of land in the kitchen garden at one end of the playground. In it the students planted cucumbers, okra, aubergine and tomatoes. When the vegetables were ripe, they were allowed to pick them and take them home to their families. PK was given the task of watering the plants. No one minded him touching the seeds and the water.

At harvest time, he was given his own basket, while the other students shared another. This, he realized, was because they did not want their vegetables contaminated by his impurity. But he did not care any more. Instead he focused on all the lovely tomatoes he would be able to take home to his mother. The thought of joining in the harvest excited him, and he ran towards the patch. And tripped. He stumbled over a water hose and into the class basket, spilling the topmost fruit. PK bent down, picked them up and put them back.

'What have you done?' the teacher exploded. 'Now they are all ruined!'

PK froze, petrified, and watched as the teacher snatched the basket from him. He sensed that something unpleasant was about to happen. Teacher raised it above PK's head and poured the tomatoes over him. A rain of round, red fruit thudded against his skull and tumbled all around, while the rest of the class stood in a ring and watched in silence. Teacher then declared that PK might as well take them all home, seeing as no one else would be able to eat them.

Crying, PK bent down, picked up the tomatoes and placed them in his basket.

Ma's face lit up when he came home with the bounty, but when he told her what had happened, she looked depressed. Maybe he would be expelled and the other villagers would harass them?

'You never know with caste Hindus,' she said. 'Sometimes they like to humiliate us in public.'

But the next day Teacher pretended as if nothing had happened. And neither PK nor the rest of the family observed any other repercussions.

PK thought about it. Teacher had explained to him that whatever he touched turned dirty. So what would happen if he touched the other students? Would they be angry? Or would they pretend that nothing had happened?

I have to try, the young PK decided.

The students were lined up in rows in the schoolyard as they did every morning. This was his moment. He made a dash for it, reached out and ran his hand over every stomach down the line. Then he ran up to his teacher and the headmaster, and patted them on their bellies.

Teacher was dumbstruck. He glared first at PK, then at the headmaster, and finally at the other children.

'Come!' Teacher cried, turning to his students. 'We are going to the well to wash. PK, you stay here. I'll deal with you later.'

Teacher used to beat the students with his cane when they broke the school rules, but PK was never whipped because Teacher did not want to soil his cane and thus spread the infection to the others. For PK, Teacher came up with a special form of punishment; he was made to stand still on the veranda with his eyes closed. Teacher then edged back and began to throw stones, small, sharp rocks that stung as they assailed his skin, and left ugly bruises.

PK cursed the teacher, but recalled his mother's words with resignation; this was their destiny, what life was like outside their home. This was how he would always be treated. There was nothing he could do about it.

Now and then it made him angry, and he fantasized about getting his revenge or having divine justice intervene on his behalf. Bittersweet thoughts came as he rode home in the afternoons, as he lay awake in the moments before dawn, as morning's first light filled the sky and his mind still clung to the events of the previous day.

And one day, divine justice seemed to play its part. Teacher had fallen asleep at his desk while the students were reading morning prayers out loud. PK could smell the moonshine on his breath and the snoring filled the classroom as Teacher's mouth gaped ever wider. Then something amazing happened, something that he would never forget. One of the pigeons that liked to sit in the beams above suddenly relieved itself. The poo fell towards Teacher's lectern, down towards Teacher's chair and, to the delight of all the children, plopped straight into his mouth. Teacher jumped up, screamed and began cursing his students, believing that one of the boys must have played a prank on him.

Had the pigeon read PK's thoughts? Whatever the case, PK took great pleasure in his teacher's shock and disgust.

The mood at school changed dramatically when the schools' inspector came to visit. His main task was to check whether the school was obeying India's anti-discrimination laws that made prejudicial treatment on the grounds of caste illegal. Dressed in a blue blazer, white shirt and white trousers with creases pressed into them, he possessed a natural authority. His smiles were polite, but they masked an iron will.

That morning, PK was instructed to join the class inside, as if his untouchability had been nothing but a bad dream. Suddenly he was one of them and allowed to play with the other students during break time. Nobody told him to go away. He felt ecstatic, liberated. But tragically, he had no idea that this was all a sham, that as soon as the inspector left, he would be cast right back into the hell of exclusion again.

Had he been a little less naïve, he would not have let himself feel such happiness.

In the evening, he told his mother how he impressed the other children by correctly answering the inspector's questions. She was visibly proud of him, and felt so moved that she cried. This made him feel better, that in her eyes he was important and valued. Years later, in his teens, he thought that perhaps his mother's tears had been shed because of the hypocrisy, that she had known all along that such treatment was only temporary, make-believe for the benefit of someone who would leave again.

He used to dream of the inspector's return. The inspector would sit diagonally behind the teacher, watching eagle-eyed over the class. Nothing escaped his gaze and he saw to it that everyone treated PK fairly. PK sat in the middle of the classroom, surrounded by the other students. He raised his hand, answered all the questions correctly and was praised repeatedly.

But such sweet sensations evaporated when he opened his eyes. He lay still, the warmth lingering in his body for just a moment longer than the dream. The pressure in his chest returned as soon as he was up and sitting out on the veranda greeting the sun, and he would replay the post-inspection ritual in his mind. It went like this: immediately after the inspector had mounted his bike and pedalled away, PK's Brahmin teacher and caste classmates would form a procession and proceed down to the reservoir to cleanse themselves with soap and water. They washed carefully and slowly, scrubbing every last trace of the stench of his presence from their skin.

The first time it happened, he went home and cried desperately.

'They were dirty,' his mother soothed. 'They needed a wash. You did them a favour, making them go for a swim. They stank!'

She would keep repeating these words until he stopped crying. Although he knew she was lying, the words were soft and warm and wrapped themselves around him like a blanket. At least someone in the world accepted him.

This charade was not performed for the inspector alone. In his third year of school, they received a visit from a British colonial official who had remained in Orissa after Independence. He and his wife stepped stiffly into the classroom, he in a dark suit, she in a floral dress. Their faces were as white and smooth as yogurt. The Brahmin girls in the class placed flower garlands around their necks. To mark the occasion, PK was once again allowed to sit with the others inside the classroom, as if the daily humiliation was nothing but a figment of his young imagination. The children stood up together and sang for their visitors, a loving family reunited.

As the British couple were leaving the classroom, the woman approached PK and patted him on the cheek. She looked him straight in the eyes and smiled.

'I can touch you, because I am also untouchable,' she said as she removed the garland of flowers around her neck and placed it on PK.

The sense of acceptance was intoxicating. This time he knew it was temporary, but he did not allow its transience to settle; no, he swatted it away like a mosquito, desperate to let the moment last a little longer.

When the British were in earshot, caste did not exist. Maybe life was better for us when they were in charge? His grandfather thought so.

He glanced at the white woman and remembered the astrologer's prediction: she will come from far, far away, from another country even. Was he destined to marry a woman in a floral dress and a face as white as yogurt?

Lotta's longing for the East only grew. *The Beatles are off to India to meditate*, the Swedish newspapers announced. She read about how George Harrison had travelled to India, met with spiritual masters, learned to play the sitar and performed an Indian song in a Hindu temple in London. She also read an interview with Maharishi Mahesh Yogi, guru to the Beatles, who said that the Fab Four had cosmic potential. India was everywhere, impossible to escape.

Lotta often thought about her grandfather, who died when she was only two. It had been his dream to travel, his greatest wish to take off for countries far, far away. He had been a weaver by trade and made friends with a travelling textile dealer from Bombay. He read books by Rudyard Kipling, Jack London and the Swedish explorer Sven Hedin, and talked constantly about having his own adventures in the Orient.

Lotta often took out the yellowed copy of the magazine *Idun* where he had circled an advert for cruises to India. Grandfather had never realized his dream. Instead, he brought the world home to him. One day he found an old incense burner at the local junkyard, which turned out to be from Persia. No one knew how it had ended up on a rubbish heap in Borås, but what did that matter? Lotta's grandfather treasured it. It was his adventure.

When he died, responsibility for looking after the censer fell to Lotta. Many years later she ended up hanging it in a niche in her home in the clearing in the woods. I'm not going to settle for a censer, Lotta said to herself, I'm going to do what Grandfather never managed.

The family home was a small, three-room apartment. They were often short of money and lived frugally. Her parents ran a fabric shop they had inherited but never really wanted, and when business dwindled, eventually they were forced to shut down. Lotta's father began working on managing the family forest, while her mother took a job as a nurse at her brother's dental practice.

It wasn't obvious from their modest lifestyle, but Lotta's family was descended from a knight. They were nobles, the von Schedvins. But what to others was a name to be proud of, to the teenaged Lotta felt like a weight around her neck. It was no fun to bear such a fancy name. Lotta wanted to be like everyone else. And yet she also felt guilty for begrudging her privileged background.

The family drove an old, rusty car that often broke down. But Lotta and her sisters wanted a horse. So the family sat down to discuss it: which was the more important investment, a horse or a car? It could not be both, it was either or. Lotta's mother held the deciding vote.

'It's more important the girls have a hobby,' she said, 'than we have a new car.'

She turned to Lotta and her sisters.

'You must learn to take responsibility for something other than yourselves.'

Lotta once saw a film at the cinema about a boy who rode around India's dense jungles on an elephant. I will have a friend like that, she thought. And before long she was writing to pen pals in Nairobi, Japan, Austria and San Francisco.

One day, a bracelet made from elephant hair arrived from Nairobi. She wore it to school the next day with pride.

India's first Prime Minister was Jawaharlal Nehru who was sworn in on 15 August 1947, the day India gained independence from the British Empire. He believed in modernity, industry, urbanization and the railways. In a speech laying out his vision for India, he talked about how the new must replace the deadwood of the past. It inspired many of PK's fellow countrymen. Indeed, his father was one of Nehru's greatest admirers, as was his school's new headmaster.

On the first day at his new job, the headmaster gathered the students in the playground to tell them about all the machines and other modern things he had seen in the city. First he described the telephone, then something so strange and magical, PK remembers it to this day.

'The locomotive,' the headmaster said with a sense of drama, 'is very long. It looks a bit like a giant snake that reaches from where I am standing here all the way over there.' He pointed to a grassy slope a few hundred metres away. 'It also moves like a snake, zigzagging through the countryside. I travelled on one for three days and two nights to get here. There was over a hundred of us sitting on it.'

PK listened carefully and imagined the train as a long, man-made snake slithering through the sand, with the people sitting astride it, as if they were riding a horse or an elephant.

'Any questions?' the headmaster said finally.

PK raised his hand.

'Can it jump up like a cobra?'

He recalled not only the cobra that had protected him as a baby, but also the one that had bitten him when he was a mere five years old. He had been so furious that he grabbed the snake, bit through its scaly skin and let it bleed until it hung lifeless in his hands. He pictured an animal many times larger than that one, shiny and powerful.

The headmaster snorted and sniffed theatrically.

'It's too heavy to jump; it's made entirely from metal,' he said.

Yes, it must be terribly heavy, PK realized. It couldn't possibly jump off the ground. But he had one more question.

'Will it come to the village?'

Now the headmaster lost his patience.

'No, it most certainly will not. It travels only on metal. Roads made of metal. And we don't have those here.'

Amazing! Roads of solid metal! Imagine how much you'd need to build a whole road! More than in all of Grandpa's arrowheads, and he had more than anyone else in the village. Perhaps if I took all of them and melted them down, it might be enough... to make a metre? Not more. And Headmaster said he travelled for three days and two nights!

He tried to imagine such a thing, but the scale of it only made him dizzy and he had to shake his head to rid himself of the feeling.

After five years, he moved on to boarding school and, just like his father and brothers, returned to his mother only one day a week.

He walked along the corridors of his new school and looked up at the ceiling. They were decorated with strange objects he had never seen before: round glass globes that hung from thin strings. A puzzling sight. Oil lamps? They were so bright! They must guzzle oil, he thought. He examined them from all angles, looking for the reservoir.

'How do the townspeople refill their lamps?' he asked his father on his first Sunday home.

Shridhar replied that he need not trouble himself with such questions, and that he would learn how everything worked in time.

'But get used to it! The Prime Minister has promised us that we will have those kind of lamps in our village soon,' he added.

From the very first day at his new school, his untouchability was apparent to everyone and his new teachers and classmates treated him accordingly. Indeed, now he carried in his pocket a folded caste certificate issued by the local authorities. This gave him access to the quotas reserved for *'Scheduled Castes'*, *'Scheduled Tribes'* and *'Other Backward Castes'*, which included untouchables and tribal people like him:

> Caste Certificate. Case Record No 44
> of 1975. Certified that Sri Pradyumna
> Kumar Mahanandia, son of Sri Sreedhar
> Mahanandia of village Kandhapada P S
> Athmallik in the district of Dehnkanal be-
> longs to schedule caste. His subcaste is Pan.

There it was, black and white proof that he was untouchable, a pariah, a second-class citizen. The certificate afforded him cheaper train tickets and would one day give him easier entry to university, that much was true. But mostly he regarded it as a stamp of his humiliation. He was nothing but a poor wretch who needed special treatment just to survive.

One of his new teachers also happened to be director of a shelter for *Dalits* (untouchables), which made him qualified to tell the young PK exactly what was expected of him and how he should behave. He was not to enter the kitchen or the dining room if anyone else was present, and, instead, should sit on the floor in the hallway and wait there for his food. The cook would come out to serve him last, and separately.

The cook came out with his pans and poured a portion

of rice, dal and vegetable curry from such a height that his ladle did not touch PK's bowl. Some days, PK was given only rice as the other food had run out. When he complained the cook only sighed, as if he was as powerless as PK in the situation.

'It's karma from your past life. You must understand and respect that,' was his only answer.

This was not the first time he had been given this explanation, invariably from Brahmins or people who had been brainwashed by them. It's not their fault, he would say to himself, they have been indoctrinated, taught to treat untouchables like lepers. But still he felt the rage swell inside him.

The school employed a Dhobi wallah, a man who washed clothes for the boarders. Except PK's. When he realized this, PK's fury turned into a deafening scream, but he was too scared to let it out. Instead, he slipped down to the riverbank, and just as he had done as a little boy with the priests at the temple, shot at the Dhobi wallah's water pots with his slingshot. Yet again, he was caught.

That week, a letter arrived for PK's father from the Dhobi wallah: 'Your son must understand and respect our rules and traditions. How would it look if he did as he pleased all of a sudden?'

Shridhar replied that he knew all about these traditions and so, no doubt, did his son. 'But,' he wrote back, 'these rules are unjust and shameful for a country that wants to be modern and compete with the successful nations of the West.'

Had the laundry man heard Prime Minister Nehru's speeches? Did he not know that the politicians in New Delhi dreamed of an India free from caste hierarchies? Had he not read Nehru's most wise pronouncement that people are creatures of free will, and are not controlled by ancient customs? Life is like a game of cards, Nehru once said, the cards you are dealt are predetermined, but life is all about your skill in the game. That is your free will.

The following week, the Dhobi wallah approached PK as he sat alone eating his meal in the corridor. 'Get your clothes for me tonight,' he whispered, 'but be sure no one sees you. I'll wash them and you'll get them back tomorrow night when the others are asleep.'

A half-victory, at least.

Indian society was full of contradictions, PK was more than aware of that. A good example was how the caste system had affected his paternal grandfather. Grandpa was a respected man when it came to secular activities. Yet it was unthinkable to the Brahmins to receive food or a glass of water that he might have touched. He was refused entry to the temple until the day he died.

The Pan had worked as weavers for hundreds of years, but his grandfather broke with tradition and took an office job in Athmallik. While the Brahmins treated him like elephant dung, the British respected him. They would do anything to annoy the Brahmins. They appointed him *chatia*, chief of the village, and tasked him with arbitrating local conflicts, as well as reporting all births and deaths and crimes committed to the colonial authorities. There was no police station or national registration office in the village, it all fell to Grandpa. The role was also punitive. If anyone violated the law it was Grandpa who beat the offender with his wooden stick, as per British orders. But most of all, this position made him an official representative of the British Empire, because the imperialists did not trust the Brahmins.

'Brahmins have so many taboos when it comes to food, as well as strange social rules, so you never know if you are insulting them. Only they seem to understand the rules,' one of the British in Athmallik was reported to have said.

The British knew that the scepticism was mutual.

Orthodox Brahmins despised the colonialists and called them Beefeaters. It was meant as an insult.

Grandpa used to tell PK how much he liked the British.

'They keep their promises; they are good people. Unlike the Brahmins, they shake hands with us. They don't mind touching us,' he said. 'Stay away from Brahmins,' he continued in his gravest tone. 'If you don't keep your distance, it will be your undoing.'

During his teenage years, PK found sanctuary and companionship in a most unexpected place: the travelling circus. They arrived one day without warning, pitched their tents, parked their elephants and built their itinerant amusement park nearby. The first evening, a queue formed for the Ferris wheel and the carousel, powered by men on reconstructed bikes. The rusty attractions squeaked, blinked and whined. It was a ramshackle affair perhaps, but PK was nevertheless impressed by the spinning, rattling machines. Yet it was the circus tent that fascinated him the most, without really knowing why. He wandered among the caravans, patting the horses and elephants and introducing himself to the jugglers and lion tamers.

PK was careful to let them know he was untouchable. Out of consideration. Then they could choose to keep their distance or shoo him away. That way he would not contaminate them.

'We don't care about stuff like that!' said one of the lion tamers.

'We're Muslims, we understand you. They treat us as if we're untouchable too,' said a juggler.

No one had ever told him that India's Muslims were treated as badly as the untouchables. Technically, Muslims did not belong to the caste system. But in fact, they too had once been low-caste Hindus who had escaped their untouchability by converting to Islam. Not that it had helped. They were excluded and humiliated just the same.

The caste system is an incurable epidemic, PK concluded.

He went to the circus after school every day. Finally, he had found a place where he was treated with common respect. The circus people were friendly, open and curious. They answered his questions and listened to his stories. It was an unfamiliar feeling. After a few days, they offered him a job. Why not? He did not care if his school work suffered. That was his way. He did not think before he acted, and good offers were so rare that he never said no.

He was flattered. For the first time in his life, he felt accepted.

For two weeks, he carried hay to the animals and ladders to the tents. He also painted their posters.

'Become our clown and join us on tour!' the circus director said to him one day.

Sure, why not? It was the beginning of the summer holidays anyway. He was given a long striped coat and a red plastic nose. He learned some tricks and sketches, and realized that it was not so hard. Best of all, the audiences laughed. The attention was easily earned and at first it was intoxicating.

The circus performers liked him. But after a few weeks, when the director asked if he wanted to join them on a longer tour of several states in eastern India, he hesitated. Something was not quite right. He had started to feel that playing the clown was the ultimate confirmation of his exclusion. What was a clown if not a failure who tried to cover up the fact by making himself a fool? He was among like-minded people, he had a job, he was even earning money, but somehow the laughter of the caste Hindus in the audience sounded scornful to him. No, he did not want to be the clown.

Exams at school were an unrelenting torture. PK would sit, staring at the questions, dumbstruck. He could barely answer a thing. Maths and physics were the worst. Had he understood nothing the teachers had been saying?

I'm untouchable, and stupid, he said to himself, full of self-pity.

If he did not pass his exams, he had no future. Then he would have to be content to clean toilets for the wealthy, or become a weaver or a brick burner, professions destined for untouchables who, like himself, were unable to make anything of their lives.

He went down to the river with the intention of surrendering himself to the rapids, to find his final relief, to obtain his own, better, revelation. He plunged forward, to end all suffering. Something else awaited him, surely.

But just as the water rushed against his skin, he had time for one thought: what would his mother say? Emotions inside him started to fight against the current that pulled him towards darkness.

He still wanted to live.

He came to the surface, swam to the shore and climbed out onto the narrow, shingle beach. Yet, an impulse told him he should try again. He jumped in, but his body struggled against the water. He surfaced. One more time, he said to himself. As his body reached the bottom of the river, he grabbed hold of a rock to keep himself underwater. He wanted this ultimate escape.

There was no turning back now.

Suddenly the stone dislodged from the riverbed and he rushed to the surface. Soaking wet and defeated, he went back to school, lay on the floor of his dormitory and stared at the ceiling.

He began processing recent events. He hated his teachers, the Dhobi wallah, the cook and the other students. He hated the way they accepted everyone's predetermined place in society. And yet, he could not shake the feeling that all these things happened for a reason. Nothing in life was meaningless. Even failure had its purpose. This sense of exclusion had its purpose, the suicide attempt had its purpose, and the stone loosening at just the right moment had its purpose too. In the search for consolation, he brought his thoughts back to the palm leaf and the horoscope. The prophecy. The woman he would marry. He imagined her, drew her in his mind. The image of a light-skinned woman took shape in the darkness before him. She was beautiful and her smile was gentle. He felt the warmth of a body as he closed his eyes, and he was convinced there was a light surrounding him. His mother. He did not know how he knew, but there was no doubting it. She was sitting on the floor beside him, stroking him.

'There now,' her voice came to him, 'they are the stupid ones; you're doing everything right. One day, you will meet the woman from the prophecy, your future wife.'

The darkness could not get any darker, but it was his mother, her light, that sustained him and stopped him from taking that plunge into the void.

It feels so nice when you sit beside me. That was the last thing he remembered saying to her that wretched evening, as he drifted off to sleep.

Military training camps were mandatory for all boys about to start their final year of secondary school. India had fought two wars with Pakistan and one with China. There were battles in humid jungles, hot salty deserts and icy glaciers. Even schoolboys had to be prepared to serve in the next conflict, because everyone knew it was only a matter of time before war broke out again.

It was time for PK to attend the National Cadet Corps youth camp in Baulpur. Over a thousand young people from all over Orissa gathered in the summer heat to practise drills and learn to shoot. They lived in tents on the banks of the Brahmani River, under mango trees weighed down with ripe fruit that fell around them in the sand. The exercises were monotonous and boring, but PK was fascinated by the uniforms, the caps and medals, and the heavy leather boots. The outfit gave him a feeling of authority.

One day, he and two other cadets were charged with guarding the tents while the others marched a kilometre along the river to cook dinner. Navy, rain-filled clouds had been hanging low above the trees all afternoon. Wind had now caught up with them. Not long after the others had left, wet hail the size of kernels of corn started swirling in the air.

The cyclone hit faster and with more force than anyone had anticipated. In less than ten minutes it had levelled the entire campsite. The dense blackness was illuminated by an occasional flash of white-blue light, and PK stumbled into a ditch he and a few others had dug that very day. A sudden gust dropped another cadet beside him. A large branch was torn from one of the mango trees like a toothpick. A smaller branch came flying and hit PK. The pain ripped into him. He looked up and saw blood gathering in pools where he lay, the scarlet liquid soaking into his clothes. Within seconds, he was drenched in it.

He looked down at his body, but he was not bleeding. That was when he realized: the blood was his friend's.

PK woke up several hours later, an irritatingly bright light hanging above him. He was lying on a hard stretcher in the hospital in Dhenkanal. He had broken his leg. His friend had been crushed by the larger branch, and was dead.

**

Before he knew it, the time for exam resits arrived. Just when all had felt so utterly hopeless, hope returned. His bad luck had finally run out. His memory began to function again. The blockage was released.

He passed. Just.

Some of what he had been taught had gone in. He was not completely useless after all.

His father saw again his chance to push PK towards the career he had chosen for him. Become an engineer, son. A job with prospects, a bright future for PK and for India, built on rationality and science, not the superstition and prejudice of the priests.

Bapa told him to apply to a science college. PK did as he was told and was accepted for the following autumn. But he soon tired of the course and instead took to drawing caricatures of the faculty staff during lectures.

'Untouchables have no brains!' his maths lecturer yelled upon discovering them.

But being thrown out of class did not cast PK into despair this time. He knew what he wanted and it was a different life to the one his Bapa had envisioned for him. He hated the natural sciences: physics, chemistry and mathematics were his worst subjects. Leave the nation building to someone else.

The same lecturer approached him the next day and gave him some sound advice.

'Pradyumna Kumar, this isn't working,' he said.

'Then what should I do?'

'Apply for art school!'

He took his teacher's advice and fled with the grand sum of fifty-five rupees in his pocket. At first he did not know where he was going, but then he remembered the Bhima Bhoi spiritual centre in Khaliapali, a couple of hours' bus ride from home. PK knew the monks welcomed lost souls like him. He was received warmly, given a straw mat to sleep on and food to eat. These people shared his values, so he took his place on the floor beside the monks, who were naked save for scraps of bark that covered their genitals.

PK was fascinated by the movement's founder, Bhima Bhoi. The monks told him that he had been an orphan boy from the neighbourhood and had formed the sect out of frustration with India's caste hierarchy, class divisions and hypocritical Brahmins. He had quickly gained followers.

The monks sang their guru's songs and recited beautiful poems that told of a just society in which people lived together and were not divided into competing factions. PK found solace in hearing his own thoughts sung out loud. Here, he was among equals. The monks felt the same way about the Brahmins as he did.

And yet, something told him he could not spend the rest of his life in meditation. The life of a monk was not for him; he needed to taste cravings and desires before he could renounce them. He would marry, the prophecy had told him so, and he wanted to see the world out there, beyond Athmallik.

He continued his journey, and stole onto a train travelling north to West Bengal. The creaking train was carrying him to a new life, and as he sat watching the world pass by the window, he recalled the headmaster who had once described trains as metal snakes. To think that he had pictured passengers astride a giant serpent as it wound its way along roads paved with metal. He laughed at his own stupidity. There was so much he had not understood.

His next destination was Kala Bhavana, an art school in the village of Shantiniketan founded by the Bengali poet Rabindranath Tagore. He checked in at the school's hostel.

Only one rupee a night for a bed? That much he could afford. But the classes were much less reasonably priced and he was forced to abandon the idea. He could not possibly write to his father for help. Instead, they told him about an art school in Khallikote, back in his home state of Orissa, designed for students from less affluent backgrounds like him.

With renewed hope, he sneaked back onto a train going south and arrived at the art school, located in an old colonial house with marble floors and a cast iron fence, nestled between towering mountains and the vast Chilika Lake.

The school was exceedingly popular because it was free. Competition for the thirty-three available places was fierce, and PK was one of hundreds of applicants. The selection process consisted of a series of tests in how well candidates could work with paints, ink and charcoal. The school set up a still life in the yard – one pot, one bunch of grapes and three mangoes – and the hopefuls formed a ring around it.

PK glanced at the other drawings and felt confident. The next day, the teachers came to announce the results. First came those who had been unsuccessful. Then, the lucky ones, graded and ranked by order of skill.

PK was placed number one.

He told no one at the art school in Khallikote that he was untouchable. And no one asked him. The teachers and students came from all over the country and they socialized together, as if neither caste nor class existed. It was a new and powerful sensation. This was a different India, and it reminded him of the itinerant Muslim circus he had briefly joined as a young boy.

Another life was possible.

That year in Khallikote was crowned by his greatest achievement so far. The teachers singled him out for his talent and in the spring invited him to apply for a scholarship to continue his studies in New Delhi. He put in an application and waited for the answer, which arrived finally to the accompaniment of the clap and roar of the summer's monsoon rains. His father, the postmaster, brought the brown, official-looking envelope home and presented it to his wife, who ripped it open, only to hand it back to her husband to read out loud.

'You got the scholarship!' Kalabati said when PK called home.

The ground beneath his feet swayed.

'You're moving to the capital,' she continued, and began to cry.

His father congratulated him, having finally given up on the idea of his son becoming an engineer.

His mother cried and refused to eat for three days before his departure. The move, for her, was a tragedy. And yet her emotions were more complex. She was also proud. Indeed, in front of the neighbourhood women, she was triumphant:

'My son is travelling by bus and train, and then he is going to fly in a silver bird over the jungle and the mountains and further away than any of you could ever imagine.'

The Transformation

It was late summer, and a perfume of fermenting fallen fruit and monsoon rain assailed his nostrils. PK was about to leave for New Delhi. He knelt before his mother and lightly brushed her feet. She cried. Holding back his own tears, he stood up, hugged her and jumped onto the cart. He signalled to the driver, and the ox responded by shaking the flies from its eyes. It then began its leisurely walk along the bumpy dirt road, the wagon PK was sitting on creaking behind it. As he made his way to the train station, PK was reminded of his horoscope: he would marry 'a girl from far, far away, from outside the village, the district, the province, the state and even the country'.

The next morning the train arrived at Bhubaneswar, the capital of the state of Orissa, an exuberant city that hit PK with a riot of new sensations. Wide, straight boulevards with traffic police clad in white positioned at the intersections. Rows of Hindustan Ambassador taxis with men dressed in starched cotton clothes sitting in the back seats. Ancient, stately sandstone temples surrounded by manicured gardens. Bazaars where the goods seemed to pour out into the streets. The delicious aroma of cooking food wafting from rows of small eateries. Cows sauntering among tinkling bicycles and roaring motorized rickshaws. And in the evenings, glistening temples, tall glass houses and lights spilling from shopfronts. It was a gleaming spectacle, an unearthly creation. How, then, would New Delhi shimmer?

He was twenty-two, or twenty-one, or possibly twenty... he did not know exactly. His illiterate mother could not be sure. Birthdays were not celebrated in his family, and there was no such thing as an identity number in the India of those days. The year was 1971: the calendar that hung on the wall at school told him so, as did the front pages of newspapers for sale by the side of the road.

His childhood had been characterized by the gradual realization of what it meant to be untouchable; the loneliness, the humiliation, which had overwhelmed the pure joy of the early years in his mother's care. Village life had been cruel. But now he stood on the threshold of a new kind of freedom, an anonymity unavailable to him back home. Everything – the houses, the streets, the city bustle, parks, temples, the vendors shouting in the markets – they were like picture-perfect visions of a dream-world.

When running to schedule, the Utkal Express between Bhubaneswar and New Delhi took two and a half days, but by the time they rolled into their final stop, they were more than eight hours delayed. What happened? The man on the bunk beneath him shrugged.

'What *hasn't* happened?' he replied. 'But we should rejoice that we have made it and not worry about the things in the past we cannot change. I mean, what can you do about it anyway?'

This sounded like good advice. Look forward, to the future. Celebrate the fact that he had made it out of the village, away from the constant bullying, to the capital, where fantasies were realized and ambitions took flight.

PK slept deeply that night, in his brave new world on the fifth floor of the Orissa Bhavan state guesthouse, the club and guesthouse for Orissans living in the city The next morning, he got up and went to the window in the hall-way. But as he stood, rubbing his eyes in the early morning light, he started to feel scared. He had fallen asleep so full of courage and wild ideas, but was awakened by fears leaping around inside his chest; a feeling that, most of all, he wanted to go back to safety, to his bed, to his village in Orissa, and to his family.

He looked out on New Delhi below: wide roads of dark smooth asphalt, white and beige hunchbacked cars, buses dented from the constant battering of dense traffic, trucks painted rainbow colours, black and yellow motorized rickshaws, swarms of motorcycles and towering buildings of concrete, steel and glass that glittered in the scorching September sun.

Will I ever feel at home here?

He started to wonder if he would even dare to go out. Maybe they would not understand him here? He spoke Oriya, his native tongue, and English, which he had learned in school. But the capital spoke mostly Hindi, of which he had gained only a working reading knowledge in secondary school; it most certainly was not a language he was comfortable speaking. *Mai Orissa se ho*. I am from Orissa. *Mai tik ho*. I am well. In Hindi, his conversation would be stiff, formal and childish.

He let his finger trail across the map from the guesthouse to the art school. It was a long way. He had no idea how to navigate the city's buses. What if he made a mistake? What if he could not find his way back? What if he was robbed or cheated? What if the city people noticed how awkward he was – unsure of himself and badly dressed – and laughed at him?

For the first week, he walked to and from the school in order to avoid having to figure out which bus to take. But he soon found it exhausting; he would have to catch a bus after all. As he approached the bus stop, fear grasped him.

The Delhi Transport Corporation's dilapidated vehicles trundled by in a steady stream, tilting heavily as cones of black smoke spewed from their exhaust pipes and passengers hung like bunches of grapes in the doorways. The bus drivers did not halt their vehicles but slowed as they approached the stop, so that people could jump on and off.

Somehow he managed to press himself onto one of the buses. After what felt like hours stuck in the depths of the sweaty human mass, he noticed the tall buildings and roundabouts were being replaced by small mud huts, then fields and thickets.

The bus, he realized, was not going in the direction of the school. He had gone the wrong way.

He jumped off at the next stop, crossed to the other side of the road and stuck out his thumb for a ride back into town.

The next day he decided to walk. The more he got to know the wide boulevards, passed the towering high rises and navigated the giant roundabouts, the less scary New Delhi became. What once seemed dangerous and hostile began to feel familiar. He felt relief. This was freedom. Here he was not the untouchable Pan boy, son of Shridhar Mahanandia, Athmallik's untouchable postmaster, and Kalabati Mahanandia, the dark-skinned tribal woman. No one had even heard of Athmallik, let alone knew where it was. He had no choice over where he had been born or his place in the caste hierarchy. But here, so far, no one had asked about any of that.

The teachers at the College of Art were modern, if not radical. They were vehemently opposed to the caste system, and just like at the art school in Khallikote, he sat inside the classroom along with the other students. High caste and low were treated the same. PK heard teachers say things like, 'The caste system is an evil that must be destroyed.'

They said it loud and proud, almost triumphantly, as if they wanted to free their young students from this obsolete and outdated culture. PK even ate with the others: in the same room, at the same table, from the same deep bowls. No one flinched as he approached and no one shunned his presence or touch. It was like living through a revolution. He walked home at night with a bounce in his step. New Delhi, the city, was his future.

The scholarship from the state of Orissa was supposed to be paid once a month and be enough to cover school fees, art materials, books, rent at the guesthouse and food. But after a few months the money stopped coming. The fifty rupees his father sent every month was only enough to cover his living costs for a few days. Someone at the government grants office was probably siphoning off the money into his own pocket. PK kept returning to the window where he was supposed to receive it and the same answer came back at him again and again:

'Sorry! No money. Come back in a month and see.'

His first year at the art college started so positively, but it quickly came to be characterized by poverty, hunger and anxiety about where he would spend the night. For the first three months he stayed with various school friends. But he did not want to trespass on their hospitality for too long. After a while, he began to sleep on the floor of New Delhi railway station along with the day labourers, the disabled, the beggars and families from the country waiting for the dawn trains. The station was full of people wrapped in blankets, big bags made from sheet metal, jute sacks filled with grain and straw, milk pots, farm implements and sometimes the occasional goat.

It was warmer and more comfortable inside the station than out on the streets. Delhi nights were not as hot as at home in the village; they were rather damp and at times bitterly cold. Moreover, he could wash in the station toilets, and therefore did not have to attend classes stinking of sweat.

Some evenings, however, he was too tired to walk all the way to the station. Those nights he crawled inside a nearby telephone booth and fell asleep.

Aged eighteen, Lotta moved by herself to London to study nursing and undertake her practical training in a local hospital. She needed no moral support, no friend to hold her hand. On the contrary. It felt liberating to go alone.

She got a job at a renowned hospital in Hampstead, where the long-term patients and staff were like family. Lotta had chief responsibility for an old and very sick man who wanted to be addressed as Sir.

'Promise me, Lotta, never, ever let yourself turn hard inside,' he said, holding her hand, on her last day.

She has carried this advice with her all her life.

In London she ate Indian food in small neighbourhood restaurants where the aroma of cumin and chilli scratched at her nose. She went to the Royal Festival Hall to see the Indian Odissi dancers with bells around their ankles and to the Royal Albert Hall to see George Harrison and Ravi Shankar's concert for world peace. For a short while, she even dated an Indian immigrant from Delhi.

And then there was the photo diary she found at the hospital. One of the pictures was of a large, stone wheel. It looked to be very old and was fringed with small sculptures of humans and elephants. She tore out the picture and stuck it to the wall above the bed in her lodgings. In the evenings she lay, staring at it.

'It's as if the wheel is pulling me,' she wrote in her diary, 'as if the image is speaking to me, deep inside, about something big that I have known, but have forgotten.'

PK started skipping class. The days he could not afford to eat, he was too tired to listen to the teachers or complete the exercises they set. Instead, he took to walking aimlessly around town. He often ended up in the area around Connaught Place, a large roundabout in the centre of the city surrounded by white colonial houses with columns and arcades. This was where the best restaurants and fanciest shops were located. In the middle of the roundabout was a park with a lawn, bushes, a fountain and a pond. In its own peculiar way, it smelled of the metropolis: the stench of stagnant water, diesel fumes and human waste mixed with the sweet incense of flowers and fruit stalls, as well as the cigarette smoke from the porters who lay on the grass inhaling *bidis*.

Next to the park, in one of the squat, white buildings, was the Indian Coffee House. This was where the capital's students, journalists and intellectuals gathered. A new kind of guest had recently started making an appearance, the European hippy. They parked their painted VW vans and converted postal trucks outside, bearing slogans, such as INDIA EXPEDITION 1973–74, NEXT STOP HIMALAYAS and OVERLAND MUNICH–KATHMANDU TOUR.

PK went to the Indian Coffee House almost every evening. He liked the atmosphere and the mix of people. Signs on the walls explained that the café was a member of the Indian Coffee Workers Cooperative. He looked up at the sepia advertisements from the 1950s: 'A fine man…' (a proud coffee farmer with a white beard and cotton cap), '… a fine coffee' (coffee beans) and finally the punchline, 'and both are Indian!' The waiters wore white pajamas with broad green and yellow belts and headdresses adorned with fans of starched, snow-white cotton. They ran barefoot on the rough coconut fibre mat and served hot, black coffee and tea with thick buffalo milk in white porcelain cups and saucers. Here, he used to sit for hours nursing a cup of tea, a pencil and a sketchpad.

He drew both waiters and guests, but especially the foreigners. Bearded, long-haired guys with cotton scarves and shirts in Indian patterns. Girls with henna-dyed hair dressed in jeans and tight T-shirts or colourful, baggy cotton shirts. Sometimes he would offer them his drawings, but he was too shy to ask for money. A cup of tea was enough. Some guests gave him a few coins nevertheless, which he used to buy paper, paints and brushes. Others asked if he was hungry, and took him to eat deep-fried samosas, pakoras, chickpeas and potatoes fried in spices and served in small bowls made of dried leaves.

When PK could no longer afford canvas and oil paint, he settled instead for thin copy paper, brown wrapping paper and black ink, which he bought for a few paisa in the narrow streets behind Connaught Place. He began to draw people on the verge of starvation, expressionistic depictions of poverty that frightened those he showed them to. For PK, famine was an important subject. The scratchy ink lines perfectly conveyed how it felt to be hungry. He was giving voice to the world's starved masses. Drawing the suffering of others alleviated his own and afforded him some moments of temporary relief.

He stopped paying his school fees, and after six months was deleted from the student register. His teachers did not mind if he continued to sit in on classes, but it felt pointless and so he stopped going. He even stopped making art altogether. He had more important things to do, such as obtain food.

After four days without eating, his stomach began cramping. It was as if a rope had been tied around it. The pain grew in intensity, surging before releasing again and turning back into a general, background ache of hunger. The physical effects were schizophrenic: he was listless and depressed one minute, lively the next. When his energy was up, his mind fixated on food. He pictured freshly made chapatis, steaming paneer and large bowls of cauliflower doused in thick, hearty sauces.

He wandered aimlessly in search of anything to eat. On one of his worst days, as he was drifting along Ferozeshah Road in Delhi's upmarket government district, he encountered a powerful aroma of spices. He could not stop himself. A wall surrounded the stately bungalow, but the gate was open. He looked inside. In the courtyard, marquees had been erected and furnished with long tables covered in red tablecloths. He saw waiters in white turbans and blue jackets running to and fro, carrying trays laden with gold-edged glasses, and musicians wearing dark blue jackets with glittering decorations as they played on scratched brass instruments.

PK was naturally cautious, he did not do things that were illegal or could get him into trouble. But hunger had crushed all such integrity. He stepped into the courtyard where the wedding party was in full swing. Hundreds of guests were chatting and eating from the buffet. Spinach lamb, cheese in red chilli sauce, tandoori chicken drumsticks with mint sauce, golden samosas, chickpea masala in yogurt, potato and cauliflower dip with cumin and coriander, chapatis, nan, pakoras...

His stomach was cramping. It was now or never. He took a plate, piled it high with food, and retreated to a corner.

He ate like a starving dog. He tried to restrain himself but could not. Worried he would be seen, he kept turning and looking around him. But no one was looking. Everyone was busy enjoying their meal.

Once his plate was empty and his stomach full, he

sneaked towards the exit. Three more steps and he would have made it, undetected. Then, a tap on the shoulder. Forceful, authoritative.

He froze, felt panic wash over him.

That's it, he thought, I'm headed for a police cell. Then I'll be sent back to Orissa, and all the shame and humiliation that awaits me there.

'Coffee or tea, sir?'

He turned. It was one of the waiters, with his gold embroidered waistcoat and white turban. At first PK did not understand what the man had said. He had not mentioned the police, he realized. Tea or coffee? Was that really what he said? A pulse of pure joy surged through him.

'No, thank you,' PK stammered. Satisfied no one else was watching, he ran out into the street and scampered between the Ambassador cars and scooters parked along the tree-lined street.

He ran up to Mandi House roundabout and then sailed along the wide avenue up towards Connaught Place. He stopped only when he was at the Indian Coffee House. Panting, he took a moment's rest. He smiled. The dull ache in his stomach was gone.

Some days he ate only jamu berries that grew on the trees along Parliament Street. In the autumn, after the monsoon rains, they dripped with purple-blue pearls. When no one picked the berries, they fell onto the pavement, staining it with pools of wine red. They were sweet and gave him energy. He washed them down with water from street taps. But eventually he became so sick that he burned with fever and his body sank from fatigue. He was unable to hold down the little food he managed to find.

He rapidly lost weight and his vision began to suffer. His whole being was now focused solely on the pursuit of stilling his hunger.

Autumn turned to winter and night temperatures sunk to just a few degrees. He slept under Minto Bridge by Connaught Place, and warmed himself beside fires of burning leaves. He had no friends left. Indifference was like an infestation crawling inside him. He could not even muster the energy to draw people in the café. Instead, he took to writing pleading letters to his father asking for money. When he heard nothing back, he wondered if his letters had arrived. Surely salvation was on its way?

When spring came, the warmth returned. Summer followed with its blistering heat. Temperatures in Delhi were approaching forty-five degrees, bubbles formed in the asphalt, pavements were deserted between dawn and dusk, and he felt sick day and night. His stomach hurt constantly and once again his thoughts turned to suicide.

Delhi, India, the world! He was more and more convinced that in actual fact, he belonged nowhere. He was poor wherever he went, equally useless and unwanted.

My birth, my whole existence, has been nothing but a mistake.

It was time to end the pain. He walked as if in a trance, his legs shaking, towards the Yamuna River. As the water once more rushed against his skin, he hoped desperately that he would never have to get out again.

But halfway to the bottom of the brown, filthy river, PK's subconscious took over. He fought his way to the surface for air, just the same as last time. His body refused to obey. It was as if his limbs were controlled by another force, which would not give up on him.

He crawled up onto the riverbank and started walking along the searingly hot streets. He did not know where he was going, but somehow he ended up at a set of railroad tracks. This was where he would put an end to it all. He would rest his head against the rails and wait.

But the metal was red-hot in the afternoon sun. He leapt up. The burn mark on his neck throbbed and he understood the folly of his plan.

Instead, he sat down.

I'll jump out in front of the next train, he said to himself. Only two steps, and it will all be over. So simple, so easy. Was that all it took to go from one world to the next?

Hours passed, but no train arrived. What was going on? Eventually a man approached along the track, cloaked in twilight. PK stopped him to ask if he worked for Indian Railways.

'Yes, I'm a train driver,' he said.

'So why aren't you driving trains?'

'Don't you read the papers?'

'No.'

'We're on strike.'

'Strike?'

'You can't sit here. Go home to your wife!'

'But I don't have a home to go to, and no wife. I'm so hungry my stomach hurts. Why do you think I'm sitting here?'

The driver shrugged and disappeared.

Moments later, a policeman came the same way.

'Go away, before I lock you up!' he shouted, shaking his wooden baton.

The next day he came across a copy of *The Times of India* and started reading. A railway strike, he read, led by George Fernandes, the president of the railway workers' union. Fernandes had persuaded several other industries to down tools in solidarity. Seventeen million Indians in total. Their anger was directed against rabid inflation, corruption, food shortages – and ultimately the Indira Gandhi government. It was potentially the largest strike in history, one columnist wrote.

I'm not the only one on the verge of collapse, he thought. The whole of India is breaking down.

Imagine, the largest strike in history had saved his life. He was not meant to die, at least not yet. A higher power had plans for him, and he had to respect that.

It could not be a coincidence that these suicide attempts repeatedly failed. He must instead focus on the prophecy. What did it say? A woman from a foreign country. He recalled the English woman who had visited his school, with her yogurt skin and floral dress. There was someone out there, looking for him. She was his destiny.

Her image grew in his mind. She became giant, occupying more and more of his waking time. And yet, it was to be an Indian friend who would pull PK out of his hunger and delirium. As for the woman from the prophecy, he would have to wait.

PK started returning to class. His attendance was sporadic at first, but then he met Narendra. They started going to the Indian Coffee House together, where Narendra would buy him tea.

'And maybe something to eat?' PK suggested.

Narendra was a medical student and, like PK, untouchable and alone in Delhi. He had gained a place to study medicine as part of the low-caste quotas, and he was doing well. Better certainly than most of the Brahmin students who refused to associate with him. The first day they met, PK told him about the hardships, the hunger and the despair of recent months. Narendra comforted him and gave him money so he could start eating more regularly, something other than the berries and leftovers that had been his only sustenance of late. After two weeks, the fever disappeared.

'You've probably been suffering from a shigella infection,' Narenda said, 'a malignant salmonella bacteria.

Otherwise known as Delhi belly.'

'What should I do?'

'It will get better by itself. As long as you eat and look after yourself.'

Just a few more weeks of hunger, one more step into the abyss, and he would have faded away forever. He was sure of this. One more week of berries and dirty water, and the illness would have broken him.

After his meeting with Narendra, even the scholarship money, which had so mysteriously vanished, reappeared. Good fortune begot more good fortune. PK's father began to answer his letters with excuses about how he had not understood how bad things had been for his son. His first letter in months contained an extra one hundred rupee note, which would be enough to cover food for a week if PK was careful.

He began to pay his school fees and attend lessons again. His desire to learn had returned and colour flooded back into PK's life. He was eager to make new friends. One of the other students had also been forced to sleep rough, and PK used to meet him under Minto Bridge. However, PK was to become close to someone who could never imagine what it meant to starve.

The majority of his classmates came from rich families. Not merely the middle class, but from the capital's political and economic elite. One had a father who was the head of the Indian Postal Service, another was the daughter of the Indian ambassador to Bulgaria, a third came from a rich Parsi family from Bombay. Her style was metropolitan, with an attitude to match.

'I grew up in the heart of Bombay,' she would say, flicking her long hair behind her as she spat chewing gum out onto the floor.

PK was shy around her. He felt inferior in her company. How could he assert himself when faced with such self-confidence and entitlement?

As long as the students spoke English with each other, he felt a bit better. On the occasions he received more money than was required to fill his stomach, he bought the *Reader's Digest*, perfect for expanding his vocabulary. In Hindi, things were more difficult, and conversation became more uncertain. He had a decent understanding of the language, but struggled with the Devanagari alphabet, which was different from the one used to write his native Oriya. He lived in constant fear that someone would point to something written down and ask him to read it out loud.

But PK wanted to overcome these feelings of inferiority and so he began chatting to a young man in the school café who looked like he might be Muslim, and therefore would not be so concerned with his caste. PK's guess turned out to be correct.

'My name is Tarique, Tarique Beg,' he said in refined English, before boasting that he had come first in the school entrance exam. 'Although, that was not my own doing,' he added.

'What do you mean?'

'Ask my father,' Tarique said, without a hint of pretension.

'Your father?'

'My father, Mirza Hameedullah Beg. Haven't you heard of him?'

'The name sounds familiar… Is he famous?'

'He's a judge of the Supreme Court.'

'Oh, Tarique, you are the son of a powerful man.'

'Yes. Unfortunately.'

'Unfortunately?'

In each other they found a common interest in philosophy. But neither was attracted to the Hindu scriptures that so enraptured the Brahmins. They spurred each other on to read the texts of Buddhism and Jainism, as well as those written by Sufi mystics. They would sit for hours in the school café, talking about human nature and how to expand consciousness, only to look up suddenly and find the janitor had come to close the school for the day.

PK was still homeless and Tarique took him in.

'You can sleep on my floor. I'm sure Father won't mind.'

The Beg family lived in a Baroque palace of twenty bedrooms and nine bathrooms among the leafy bungalows of south Delhi. Shortly after PK moved into Tarique's room, the family hosted a lavish wedding party for his sister. The buffet table in the garden groaned under the weight of the delicacies that had been specially prepared. Large sections of India's political elite were in attendance, and even Prime Minister Indira Gandhi made an appearance. Needless to say, PK was not welcome. As the guests arrived through the main entrance, he lay on the floor in Tarique's room, which had been locked from the outside. Tarique had promised to return with a smuggled plate of food. PK felt like a mutt, waiting to be fed.

He listened to the murmur of conversation and the jangling of music coming from outside. He heard laughter and smelled the delicious aroma of spices. Finally, late in the evening, Tarique came.

He lived in Tarique's room for months. Despite the breathtaking discrepancy between their family backgrounds, they had so much in common. But philosophical discussions could only take place after PK had dealt with a more pressing question: 'Do you have anything to eat?' When, many years later, PK and Tarique resumed contact again via email, this was Tarique's prevailing memory of his poor young friend: 'You were constantly hungry, it was the first thing on your mind.' Only once the roar in PK's stomach had been quelled could they deal with the Buddha.

Tarique's father became increasingly sceptical of his son's impoverished friend. The judge was polite to PK, greeted him respectfully as befitted a well-mannered former student of Trinity College, Cambridge. He never said directly that PK was not welcome, not to his face anyway. But Tarique was often forced to endure long interviews with his father, in which he begged for mercy on PK's behalf.

Tarique told PK that his father was trying to convince him to make friends with the children of better-known and wealthy families. The situation became more pressing as each day passed. Eventually, Tarique lied to his father and said PK had moved out. Tarique sneaked plates of food to him from the family dining room. When Tarique's father came from his side of the palace to talk, PK hid in the wardrobe. He felt so ashamed, standing in the dark and listening to the rumble of the judge's voice outside.

He kept himself hidden from Tarique's father and the rest of the family throughout the spring of 1973. Quite how long he stayed, none of them can remember. Perhaps he moved out one day in May, when the mercury was about to rupture the glass thermometers and the asphalt on the Connaught Place roundabout had turned sticky like English toffee. Maybe it took until the summer monsoon pulled in the lead-coloured clouds, swept the streets of the capital clean and cooled the hot air. No one can say for sure. But Tarique never threw him out. He was the best friend a person could hope for.

During those hot spring nights on Tarique's floor, PK was assailed by terrible nightmares. He usually forgot what they were about as soon as he awoke, but the horror and fear lingered. One night, soaked with sweat, he opened his eyes and saw his mother approaching in the pitch black of Tarique's room. A faint grey dawn glow clung to her and her sari was wet and pulled tight around her body, as if she had just come back from her morning wash in the river. As usual, her black hair was damp and she carried a clay pot filled with water on her head.

How can Ma be here? In New Delhi?

'Everything will work out,' she said sombrely and placed the pot on Tarique's floor.

'My journey is over now,' she continued. '*Sona Poa*, you must take care of your sister. Promise me that. You have only one sister!'

He opened his eyes and was wide awake. There was no one else in the room, apart from Tarique who lay asleep, his chest rising and falling with heavy breaths. It was half past three in the morning. But he could still feel his mother's presence, soothing him, just as she had done all those years ago when he slept in her arms. But then he knew: she was telling him that something was wrong. The more he thought about those final words, the harder his heart thumped in his chest. He could not remain on the floor as if nothing was happening, much less go back to sleep.

He packed his bag, crept out of the house without waking Tarique, and made his way to the railway station. He jumped into the carriage where passengers with unreserved tickets crowded onto wooden benches. Less than an hour after he had awoken from his dream on Tarique's floor, he was on his way back home.

After three days, four changes and a long bus ride along potholed roads through the forest, he was standing outside his childhood home in Athmallik.

Shridhar came out, surprised to see his son standing before him with crumpled clothes and messy hair, sticky with sweat and dust.

'How did you know that your mother is sick?' he asked.

'I didn't,' PK replied. 'Or... well, I did. I dreamed it.'

'Kalabati knew you were coming,' Shridhar said. 'We didn't believe her. I tried to persuade her otherwise. But she is stubborn. She kept saying, "I know my son is on his way." Come, your mother is waiting for you. Our bird is about to fly her cage forever.'

The family gathered around Kalabati's bed. She was only about fifty, her hair was not yet grey, but a recent stroke had robbed her of her previous sparkle, or at least that was the explanation given by the medical centre in Athmallik.

Kalabati stared at PK. Then she spoke without any unnecessary greetings: 'You must never drink alcohol, and never make your future wife unhappy.'

Then, just like in his dream, she added: 'And you must take care of your sister. Promise me. You only have one sister.'

The conversation with her son was to be her last great effort. Her condition worsened rapidly. By that afternoon, as PK gently poured water into her half-open mouth, she could no longer swallow. A gurgling emanated from her throat, followed by exhausted splutters. Laboriously, she turned onto her side. Her eyes could no longer focus and her breathing was slower and lighter.

And then, Kalabati died.

That same afternoon, Shridhar sent a message to the village carpenters that he needed a load of wood for the cremation. PK and his father carried her body down to the river, helped by his younger brother Pravat. They placed the stretcher on the sand and squatted by the edge of the bank where the ground fell steeply to meet the water below.

There they waited patiently. The sun went down, the wind stirred and clouds clogged the sky. Rain began to fall and the ground shook as thunder and lightning cut through the darkness, just as it had all the other monsoons that had come before. PK sat with his mother's body in his lap, afraid that the storm would take her from him. He held tightly to her feet, as if it would stop her from leaving him.

The night was as black as soot, but in the flashes of lightning he caught glimpses of his mother's pale face and stiff, grey feet. Several of the untouchables gathered to witness the upcoming cremation, only to leave in the belief that evil spirits had taken possession of the riverbed.

But PK was not afraid. He felt sad, but also secure. Peaceful.

At last, the carpenter arrived. But he approached on foot. They had broken down a good distance from the river, and he was unable to deliver the wood. There could be no cremation that night.

'You can't sit all night in this storm with your mother's body in your lap. She'll begin to rot soon,' his father said.

PK and his brother had to do something. They climbed

down the sandy slope to the edge of the water and there the three of them dug a half-metre hole with their bare hands. They gently placed Kalabati inside it. In the absence of a cremation, they would have to settle for a sand burial, in the hope that the river would take her body into its swirling embrace.

His father and little brother showed no emotion, but PK sobbed. Then, suddenly, he jumped into the grave on top of his mother. 'Bury me with her!' All was quiet for a few seconds. The rain whipped against them, but no one said a word. Silently, Shridhar pulled his son up and onto the sandy bank. Then he began to shovel the sand over his wife's body.

PK set off for Delhi the next morning. He did not stay to attend the funeral, which was to be held a few days later, as, according to tradition, he would have had to shave his hair. PK did not want to get rid of the long, flowing locks that had taken an age to grow, inspired by the hippies he had met in the Indian Coffee House. Moreover, he had already said his goodbye to his mother on the riverbank.

The invulnerability he had felt as his mother lay in his lap quickly dissipated, replaced by a feeling of emptiness as the train rattled across the Ganges plain on its way back to his life in the city.

Invisible bands had been broken, he would later write in his diary. 'Sometimes we fly, but we always land back in our mothers' laps. Now she's gone I have no ground to stand on. Life is unstable. The ground is collapsing under my feet. I'm falling.'

Term ended, and PK and Tarique decided to take a trip together. They had talked about visiting PK's father and brothers, and also wanted to make a pilgrimage to the holy sites of Buddhism.

They began with PK's village. They hitchhiked around Orissa and called in on a dejected Shridhar, who had not yet recovered from his wife's death, before taking a winding bus up to the slopes of the Himalayas and the Kathmandu Valley in Nepal. It was the first time either of them had left Indian soil, the first time they had seen snow-capped peaks or trampled through puddles covered in a thin film of ice.

Everything sparkled; colours were bright and distinct. The sky was so clear and blue, there was none of the dirt-brown haze that hung over New Delhi. One afternoon, as PK sat drawing trees in Kathmandu's Ratna Park, a man approached. 'Namaste,' he said politely, bringing his hands together and bowing his head. 'Do you draw people?'

PK hesitated. 'Yes. Sometimes.'

The man's face was marked by a straight nose and framed by a Nepalese style of hat that looked like a forage cap. His profile was distinctive, and thus not too difficult to capture. The man seemed satisfied with the picture and asked if he might buy it for a few rupees. This aroused the curiosity of a passing man who asked if PK might do a drawing of him too. As the sun disappeared behind the peaks of the Himalayas, a crowd had formed an orderly queue as paying customers waited to have their portraits done.

After four hours of drawing, his right arm ached, but his pockets were bulging with coins and crumpled bills.

The money paid for four days of breakfast and dinner at the cafés of Freak Street. Just being able to pay his own way and not have to rely on Tarique's generosity was liberating. PK could feel the weight of his poverty being lifted. Things might work out, after all.

Tarique and PK were like two exotic birds among the Western hippies who frequented two of Kathmandu's most popular cafés, Patan and the Snowman. An untouchable jungle boy and the son of a rich Muslim judge. Neither of them belonged with the adventurous children of Europe's middle classes. The young hippies shunned the West while PK and Tarique longed for it. For PK's part, it was not the wealth or their advanced technology he so admired, but the fact that they did not seem to have Brahmins, or a caste system. They probably have poor people in Europe too, he thought, but they can't be as oppressed as India's untouchables, surely?

Nevertheless, they did their best to fit in with the Europeans, who spent their evenings disparaging materialism, smoking hashish and eating apple pie. The Westerners must have found them fascinating, natives dressed in jeans, well read and well spoken.

Things were about to change radically for PK. For the first time, he was making money. Their last evening in Kathmandu was going to be his new beginning, the start of a life in which he would never again have to starve.

Back in New Delhi, Tarique told PK he was too scared to have him back in his house, for fear of his father's wrath. PK did not blame him. He would have done the same. But this meant that once again, he was homeless. Some nights he slept with friends from the art school, other nights he was back on the stone floor of the train station. Despite his optimistic mood only weeks before in the cafés of Nepal, the depression returned with force. He felt doomed to these endless setbacks.

But this time, he had a way out. He was going to become a commercial artist. And he knew the perfect place to set up shop: the fountain in Connaught Place Park in the centre of Delhi.

Guests from the Indian Coffee House often came to watch as PK made his portraits by the fountain. Every afternoon a crowd formed around his newly purchased easel.

But the spectators also began to attract the police.

'Sir, honourable Police Commander, please, I need to earn my living somehow, right, sir? Do you not agree, sir?'

Most of the police officers turned out to be decent, however, or at least open to bribes. The Chief of Police used to be satisfied with a portrait.

'Then you don't have to pay the fine,' he would say.

The walls of the police station began to fill up with PK's pencil and charcoal drawings.

When this did not work, he would be taken to the police station. But PK did not complain. He quickly understood the advantage of not demanding instant release. This way, he got a warm cell, was offered food and even got to shower. He would then be free to go the next morning, clean and rested.

He began cooperating with one of the police officers in particular, who came to arrest him only after his peak hours were over for the day. Their agreement: PK got a bunk in a cell, and the officer took fifty per cent of his income. This lasted for some time, until the officer's colleagues began to be suspicious and PK's policeman felt obliged to ask him to lie low for a while.

But PK had to make money, so he moved his business out to the area around the airport. Which was where he happened to be working on Republic Day, 26 January 1975.

People had lined the main boulevard from the city centre out to the airport. Vehicles were banned and police formed human chains to prevent the crowds from surging into the road. People moved as one, shoulder to shoulder, facing the direction of the terminal. Some carried placards, others flowers. PK saw men with cameras and notepads. Suddenly a wave went through the crowd, someone was pushed and fell, and shouts rose up, only to be drowned out almost instantaneously by an excited murmur. Who was everyone waiting for?

Two police jeeps appeared, and then two more. The cortége crept towards them, making a show for the audience. The murmur grew louder. PK penetrated the crowd and found a spot with a good view. That was when he caught sight of the woman in the jeep. Her skin shone milky white in the strong, summer sun.

She has come from somewhere far away, he realized.

'Valentina, you're our hero!' someone shouted.

PK was pressed in between a group of tall Sikhs and a class of schoolchildren. The children cheered. PK joined them. As he had no flowers, he began instead to sketch the woman. She had dropped from the sky, landed at the airport, and was now being transported like a queen towards the centre of the city. He pushed past people to get closer. The jeep had stopped. PK reached over and tried to hand the sketch to the woman in the open top car, but a security guard blocked him with his wooden truncheon. The man took the drawing instead, looked at it, and smiled. He passed the picture to the woman. PK saw her examine the portrait, then look up at the guard, who pointed to PK. He met the woman's gaze. She leaned forward and murmured something to the guard, who turned to PK.

'Madame wants to speak with you,' he said.

'Now?'

'No, you idiot! How would that work?'

He was given a piece of paper with an address. *The Embassy of the Union of Soviet Socialist Republics, Shantipath, Chanakyapuri,* it said.

'Tomorrow at noon. Bring your picture and don't be late,' the guard added brusquely.

He approached the Soviet Embassy in the tidy diplomatic quarter of Chanakyapuri. Indian government officials and Russian diplomats were standing at the entrance, surrounded by journalists and photographers. There she was, a little further inside the building, deep in the pit of people and framed photographs of Soviet leaders. A guard shoved him towards her, she took his hand and thanked him in broken English.

'A beautiful portrait,' she said, introducing herself, 'Valentina Tereshkova.'

'A beautiful face,' replied PK.

Who was she? They smiled together at the cameras. Tereshkova? He had never heard the name before. There was only time to exchange a few pleasantries. With so many diplomats and journalists in the room, he could not add anything personal, like a question: are you married?

Instead, he was hit with questions from curious journalists as soon as he came out.

'Who are you? Where are you from?' they wanted to know.

PK asked the journalists to tell him instead who Valentina Tereshkova was.

'Oh my God, how ignorant can you be? The world's first female cosmonaut!' cried one of the journalists.

PK was delighted. He did not need to know more. Outer space! That was enough for him. He answered their questions, telling them about the village in the jungle and his tribal mother and untouchable father. The reporters scribbled intensively. Indians love a feel-good story and the journalists knew this dark-skinned young man was gold. PK, the poor, low-caste boy from the jungle, had been given the chance to meet the world's most famous female cosmonaut.

***

That evening, he sat at the coffee shop on Connaught Place and thought of Valentina Tereshkova. By now he had read the day's newspapers. Once a textile factory worker, on the morning of 16 June 1963, Valentina had donned her spacesuit and stepped up onto the bus that was to take her out to the launch site, the newspaper said. The rocket had roared and the controls had buzzed. After a two-hour countdown, the engines were fired and they had lift off. Valentina, codenamed Gull, began her journey up into Earth's orbit. She spun forty-eight times around the planet over two days, twenty-two hours and fifty minutes, before coming down again in a small cone of steel equipped with parachutes, and landing on the barren steppes of Kazakhstan. Back on Earth, she continued as a researcher in aeronautics, and became a member of the Supreme Soviet of the Soviet Union and the Central Committee of the Communist Party.

And now she was in India.

There was something otherworldly about a woman travelling in a vehicle out in space. What could it mean? He thought of the elusive goddess Durga, usually described as a saviour figure, the mother of the world who fights the demons that threaten the divine order. Durga is mostly depicted standing on a severed buffalo's head while carrying the sort of large weapons usually sported by male gods, or else she is portrayed riding a lion or a tiger.

Valentina Tereshkova had escaped Earth, but had come back again. A woman from a place beyond everything. A woman riding a roaring lion, a fire-breathing rocket. A cosmonaut.

Maybe she was the woman the astrologer had prophesied?

He fantasized about a life spent with her. But it was hard to imagine. He pictured himself following her back in a motorcade as it drove into the sunset, then arriving, after a long journey, in her hometown in the Soviet Union. She stood beside him in a floral dress, he wore a dark Western-style suit. When he tried to envisage their surroundings, things became more diffuse, the emotions weaker, the colours paler. He had never seen a Soviet city, let alone a cosmonaut's house. He did not know how they lived in the Soviet Union, what their food tasted like, the shapes of their cars or the height of the trees.

He read about the poor Kazakh villagers who had gathered around her capsule upon landing. The woman in the spacesuit stood face to face with the hungry, hollow-eyed shepherds and farmers.

'Wait!' she said, and turned back to the capsule where she rooted around for some small packages, boxes of biscuits and other food left over from her trip into space.

'Here, take this!' she said, and offered what she had.

She was later chastized by the Space Agency welcoming committee; she should not have given away her space food.

PK imagined Valentina landing her spaceship in Athmallik and handing out the packages of dry food to the needy. The thought made him warm inside, because he knew there were good people in the world and Valentina was one of them. She did what she could to reduce human suffering.

But the dream was fading. He knew deep down that she was not the woman from his prophecy, she was not his wishing star. Such ridiculous thoughts! He walked through the dark, deserted streets of the city in search of a cardboard box or telephone cubicle to sleep in.

The next day he scoured the newspaper stands that lined the pavement outside the railway station. *The Navratnam Times. The Times of India. The Hindustan Times. The Hindu. The Indian Express.* What they had written about him?

'Is that you, in the papers?' a chai man nearby asked.

'Yes, that's me,' he said as he paid the man thirty paisa and received a rough terracotta cup of steaming tea. The man looked up at him from where he was squatting by his dented aluminium kettle, which bubbled over a crackling fire. He was impressed.

PK bought *The Times of India* and flicked through its pages.

There they were, on page twelve. Valentina and PK, standing in the embassy. *Boy from jungle meets woman from outer space*, the headline read.

His head was filled with noise. His life story, not someone else's, right there in the paper.

That day PK was the talk of Delhi's bus queues and tea-shops. Several newspapers carried the story. People greeted him as he made his way from the station, taking his usual detour through the bumpy main street of Paharganj market. People stopped and asked if he was well as he walked past peeling façades and loosely hanging billboards and out onto the wide Panchkuian Road towards Connaught Place.

After a summer working in Stockholm, Lotta was back in England, on the south coast, learning English. As part of her studies she had to prepare a special project, and hers was going to focus on India, obviously. She took the train up to London from Portslade-by-Sea and made her way to the Commonwealth Library. Over the course of a few weeks she worked intensely, putting together an exhibition about the tribal people of Orissa and their ceremonial murals in particular.

As she sat looking at the pictures of Indian ikat fabrics, she thought the patterns felt familiar. Then it hit her. They looked just like some of the material used in the traditional festive clothing of Sweden. In fact, they were almost identical to the ones made in Toarp, a small community on the outskirts of Malmö. How could Indian and Swedish fabric be so similar?

Everything happens for a reason.

India had problems. Inflation was out of control and un-employment was on the rise. PK read in the newspapers that Prime Minister Indira Gandhi had described the situation as 'increasingly difficult to contain'. The Hindu right wing threatened to incite religious strife.

PK, however, walked his usual route between the station where he slept and the fountain where he made his living.

A neatly dressed man stood to the side as PK was drawing another customer.

'A portrait, sir? Ten minutes, ten rupees!' PK said without looking at him.

'Not for me,' the man answered. 'Come, so we can talk undisturbed.'

'Why?'

'Our great President, the honourable Fakhruddin Ali Ahmed, wants to invite you to dinner. He also wants you to do his portrait,' said the man, who introduced himself as the President's secretary.

A few days later, PK was driven to the Presidential Palace in a white Ambassador with red lights on the roof and sirens blaring.

Originally built by the British for the last viceroy, the Presidential Palace was an imposing sandstone building that radiated power and strength.

He was received by the Presidential Guard, which consisted of a few sturdy Sikhs in turbans. They could crush me with one hand, PK thought, as he was ushered inside. Everywhere he looked, there were gold, mirrors and chandeliers, the shine of the old Empire. PK was impressed. He'd never seen anything like it, except in pictures. It was almost unthinkable that he, of all people, should be here, in the centre of power in the middle of the nation's capital, about to meet the President.

He put his palms together and bowed deeply as a gesture of respect. The President sat next to a small round table on which stood a vase of flowers. PK began work immediately. The secretary glanced at his stopwatch. 'Tell me when you are done,' he said.

Thirteen minutes later, PK called 'stop' and the secretary pressed the button. The President looked at the drawing. He sat studying it for a long time without saying anything. Then he turned to PK.

'Lovely,' he said.

The President then started to make jokes. He had a laugh like a scooter start engine. Just like any other ordinary Indian uncle.

As PK was leaving, he heard the President say to his secretary: 'Don't forget to send money to my daughter.'

PK liked him; the President of India seemed to be a loving parent, worrying about how his children were getting on now they had left home. It made him seem more human. As he left the palace, PK was met by a wall of shouting journalists and flashing cameras. The press wanted to know what the President had said.

'He said he had to send money to his daughter,' PK replied, believing the journalists would interpret it the same way he had, that the President was a caring, likeable man.

But the reporters did not find it nearly so charming.

'He should be worrying about the country, not his family,' one said.

'India's future is more important than his daughter,' complained another.

'You get the leaders you deserve,' said a third.

The next day, all the major newspapers published articles about his visit to the palace, illustrated with photos of the President, PK and his portrait. The fact that the drawing had taken only thirteen minutes to complete was a major focus of the reports, as if he had been an athlete, not an artist.

In the spring of 1975, the police were becoming ever more aggressive in their treatment of crowds. The government was afraid that the political unrest might escalate into violence, riots and rebellion.

PK had installed a sign at the fountain: *Ten rupees, ten minutes.* The queues grew. He started to become so popular that the police saw him as a security risk. The chief of the Connaught Place station came to see him personally, declaring: 'This cannot continue!'

So they took him in again.

After he was released early the next morning, he went to the art school, his stomach full and body rested, and then straight back to the fountain to take up where he had left off the night before.

In addition to the commissioned portraits, PK hung landscapes and expressionistic oil paintings from his starvation period on display. These paintings grew in number. Every evening, between six and nine, the fountain and the sunset mirrored each other in the most beautiful spectacle PK had ever seen. The last rays of the day created rainbows out of the atomized water droplets. This was the most inspiring gallery possible for his art.

Gradually, the police grew politer in their dealings with him. They still arrested him on occasion, mostly for show, so that people knew they were taking action. Increasingly, however, they left him in peace. The newspaper articles earned him the moniker 'the Fountain Artist'. The teachers at the art school admired his industriousness and gave him encouragement. Students who had not previously noticed him wanted to be friends. Within the space of a few weeks he had gone from a nobody, to a celebrity. Everybody loves success.

After the meetings with the cosmonaut and the President, he began appearing in the media on a weekly basis it seemed, as he was interviewed for television, radio and magazines. He became the subject of conversation from the country's slums to the parties of the elite, and the queues around his easel grew ever longer. His reputation spread, reaching the centre of power, and two MPs, who had seen his picture in the paper, invited him to the Constitution Club of India on South Avenue, close to the Prime Minister's residence.

That was where they were sitting and talking when Parmeshwar Narayan Haksar happened to see him.

Haksar was Indira Gandhi's principal secretary. The government was in trouble and Haksar knew they needed good publicity. PK could be just the right person, went his thinking. He came from the very bottom of society, but he also personified the drive that Haksar thought many privileged Indians lacked. PK was a victim of society's evils, everything that Indira Gandhi and the Congress Party wanted to change about India. The untouchables represented a large potential voter base, a fifth of the country's population. If Indira Gandhi could win their support, she would be able to implement the drastic measures she was hoping for and still win the next election.

PK quickly realized that Haksar was an important person whom Indira trusted. He was her media adviser, personal think-tank and political strategist all in one, and a persistent advocate of more socialist government policies. He belonged to the inner circle of radical Brahmins from Kashmir. Some political commentators claimed that Haksar was behind the government's nationalization of the banks and the excommunication of certain emblems of capitalism such as Coca-Cola.

Haksar introduced himself and asked: 'Would you agree to do a portrait of the Prime Minister?'

'Yes, sir,' PK replied, jumping up from his chair.

'Where can I reach you? Phone number?'

'Sir, I have no phone.'

'Address then?'

'I sleep one night at the railway station, the next at the police station, sir.'

'Shhh!' Haksar whispered. He leaned closer. 'I'll arrange somewhere for you to stay.'

Indira Gandhi was an impressive woman. Motherly and authoritative, and yet jolly at the same time. She made jokes about the recent news and the objects that decorated the Prime Minister's residence. PK did not fully understand them, but her entourage laughed and PK decided it was better to laugh along too.

He had imagined she would be tall, that he would have to crane his neck to speak to her. But she was barely five feet seven, around the same height as him, but with a fine womanly figure and beautiful eyes. Just like a movie star.

Indira asked PK politely where he came from and about his future plans.

His voice trembled as he answered.

'Orissa, I come from Orissa, but now I go to art college here in Delhi,' he said, trying to sound dignified.

'I see,' Indira said, somewhat distracted. She paused and looked at the flowers in the pots by the window.

'Hello,' she said, turning to the man standing by the door. 'You must remember to water the plants. Don't forget to water the plants.'

She then sank back into her ruminations.

Indira and PK looked through his portfolio of oil paintings, charcoal drawings and pencil sketches. The Prime Minister had attended Tagore's art school in Shantiniketan, this much PK knew, so she had a genuine appreciation of art. She flipped through his work, registering a partial interest with a few nods and ah-has.

'This one is nice,' she said, holding up a drawing, 'but the others... Hmm, well, you will have to practise more. That's the only way to get better.'

She praised him nevertheless and said she earnestly hoped that he would become famous. 'You deserve it.'

They then went into another room to eat lunch, served by uniformed waiters. They sat at the table, Indira Gandhi, the world famous Prime Minister, and PK, the homeless jungle boy. But Indira did not know that PK slept in the railway station; Haksar had not told her.

If only Ma could see me now.

He glanced at Indira as they ate. She peeled her own cooked potatoes. Strange. Couldn't the servants do that for her?

After this first meeting with Indira Gandhi, PK went straight to Orissa Bhavan. He was going to meet a friend from school who was working as a cook in the clubhouse. PK was looking forward to being given another meal, but was greeted by a crowd of strangers as soon as he stepped through the door. People looked at him differently now, he could sense it. They were curious, expectant. What was he going to say? Now they assumed it would be interesting.

'I've prepared a special meal for you, PK,' his friend said and bowed deeply as if he was talking to a state official.

'Who are *they*?' PK asked and pointed at a group of men nearby.

'Journalists,' his friend replied and smiled. 'They want to know what she said.'

A journalist from *The Navbharat Times* approached and asked for an interview. PK responded willingly to his questions. He liked the attention, and the fact that they were asking him, of all people, about the Prime Minister. It made him feel important. But the journalists also seemed to want to make the meeting more remarkable than it really was.

In reality, it had been nothing more than a conversation about art with an influential woman. Not just any woman, to be sure. But it was not that amazing, was it?

He had been nervous and unsure of himself during that first meeting with Indira Gandhi. Indians worshipped the Prime Minister as if she was a goddess and he had not known how to behave.

But there were to be more meetings with Indira. Three in all. And it was all down to Haksar. The second time they met, his fear eased and she seemed like a genuinely good person. He did not need to be afraid of her.

On the third occasion, he allowed himself to be photographed in the gardens of her residence together with the Prime Minister and a group of untouchables from Orissa. Indira's photographer took the pictures and they appeared on the front pages of several newspapers the next day. She stood in the middle in her lion-yellow sari, her undulating hair shimmering from a distinguished light grey to black, while the untouchables squatted in the grass, as if they were her disciples.

After all these meetings, rumour spread back home in Orissa that the Prime Minister, the 'Mother of the Country' as she was known, had adopted PK. He was no longer the son of Kalabati, the tribal woman who had been dead and buried for several years. He was born of Indira Gandhi now, even though he was not in need of a new mother. Perhaps in these troubled times, Indira Gandhi's government needed him more.

Lotta was not the type to obsess over setbacks. They were nothing more than passing rain clouds that she let float by as she went in search of sunshine. What was important was the here and now. There was real misery in the world to be sure, but still, it was best not to over-identify with the darker aspects of life. Many people got stuck reliving their past again and again, as if only comfortable when in pain.

She started practising yoga, and in it found a philosophy perfectly suited to her personality. The movements and breathing techniques were grounded in an idea she had already embraced: it takes guts to change yourself, but you cannot be a slave to your mind forever.

Everyone wants to find happiness, but it is difficult to live by such principles. We need reminding of them every day, so as not to stagnate, she told herself.

But how was it possible to be happy in the knowledge of the way people treated each other and the horrible injustice of the world? Yes, it was important to be politically engaged, and yet she could not bring herself to be so. There are many different and equally valid opinions. No ideology should claim to be absolutist. She belonged to no religion, wore no badge to declare her political allegiance. She could no more call herself Christian, Hindu or Buddhist, than conservative, liberal or socialist.

Take a little bit from all of it.

Despite her Christian upbringing and a natural affinity for yoga and the Eastern philosophies, Lotta was critical of organized religion. She was a humanist. That was enough. Everyone had within them the same energy, regardless of ancestry or skin colour. It was simply impossible to be racist, thought Lotta.

The money PK earned from his portraits went towards paints and canvases, which enabled him to make ever larger artworks with a greater variety of techniques and subject matter. Most were sold to foreign tourists by the fountain or inside the Indian Coffee House.

Haksar had promised to arrange an apartment for PK, but was taking his time. In the meantime, PK rented a small room in Lodi Colony, one of the city's more affluent suburbs just south of a large, leafy park, home to a grand mausoleum to the medieval sultans of Delhi. But his new accommodation was anything but grand. The bare room contained only a bed and a bedside table, three hooks screwed into the unpainted cement wall for hanging his clothes on, and a couple of square metres of floor space for hosting his homeless friends.

He was starting his third and final year at art school and was often the talk of the canteen. The other students increasingly regarded him as some sort of guru. Even the teachers and experienced visiting artists more than twice his age came to ask him for advice. They wanted to know about technique, what materials he used, whether his parents were famous artists, about his thoughts on art in general and what Indira Gandhi was really like in person.

One of the students from the year below was especially keen to make contact. She did not say much at first, but PK thought he could sense she wanted something. Finally, she gathered her courage and introduced herself.

'My name is Puni,' she said softly, as if ashamed to be so forthright.

But her question was surprisingly direct:

'Will you have lunch with me?' she asked.

'Yes,' PK responded without thinking. He rarely said no

to an invitation. But Puni seemed to doubt his sincerity.

'I'm not disturbing you, am I?' she asked anxiously.

'Yes,' he replied. 'You are a bit! I'm in the middle of work. But it's a nice distraction to be invited to lunch by you.'

After a pleasant meal in the school cafeteria, she invited him home.

'My mother wants to meet you,' she said. 'Can you come by on Sunday?'

'Your mother? Why does she want to meet me?'

'She wants you to do her portrait.'

The traffic, which consisted mainly of Ambassador cars, imaginatively painted trucks and worn-out buses, crept like cold syrup. It mixed lugubriously with a stream of bi- cycle rickshaws pouring out of the narrow streets around the Jama Masjid market. PK sat on the passenger bench in the back of a pedal rickshaw, gazing out at the chaos and the crowds. It was a wonderful feeling. He had never before allowed himself the extravagance of being driven by a bicycle taxi, to sit and watch as a man carried him forward on pure strength alone. He thought of the land- owners, merchants and Brahmins accustomed to having servants wait on them, as if they somehow deserved it. In that moment, he felt he deserved it too, to have a man do the heavy work for him.

They snaked through the increasingly dense throng at Chandni Chowk, past jewellers, fabric shops, signs ad- vertising chilled tap water and photographers with their wooden box cameras taking pavement portraits. The rickshaw driver swerved into alleys, dodging cyclists, wandering goats, other bicycle taxis, wobbly cows, yap- ping dogs, women in grey scarves and men with crocheted skullcaps. They passed holes in the walls and jute sacks filled with flour and chillies. It was an exhilarating sight.

Delhi's markets still felt like exotic fairytales for the boy from the jungle. The city smelled of history and power, but also overcrowding and poverty. The air stank of the black, sticky mud that festered in the open sewers, but it was also mixed with the seductively sweet scent of patchouli smoke from courtyards flaunting their syrupy mangoes and figs.

Finally, he had arrived. He got out, paid a handsome tip to quell his bad conscience, and knocked on the old wooden door.

'Welcome!' came a voice from behind the door. It was Puni.

She looked tense. 'Can I get you something to drink?'

'Water is fine,' PK replied.

She giggled. She was nervous, PK realized.

'Tea or coffee then.'

'Maybe later.'

All was quiet. He looked around. The walls were decorated with pictures of India's superstar actors and actresses, and fashion magazines covered the coffee table. Puni returned with a glass of water on a tray. A smell filled the room. She must have made a detour via the bathroom and sprayed on more perfume. The sweet scent of jasmine and roses tickled his nostrils. He looked at her. She looked different. She was wearing a shiny salwar kameez, her cheeks were daubed with rouge and her lips painted red. She wanted to look older, gone was the sincere and undecorated art student.

He gulped down the water.

'Where is your mother? I can start right away.'

'Oh, my mother had to leave just before you arrived. Something came up... something urgent at work.'

He suspected at once something was not right.

'Wait, she'll be back,' Puni said in a gentle voice.

But he was uneasy and decided he had to leave at once.

'Sundays are my best day at the fountain. The customers

will be waiting. I have to go make my living. Goodbye!' he said and left.

'Good morning!'

He recognized the voice behind him. He turned in the corridor. It was Puni again.

'My mother bought two tickets for the movies tonight, the late show at the Plaza. But she changed her mind and doesn't want to come with me. Do you want to come instead?'

'What film?'

'I don't know, but my mother is very selective.'

'Let me think about it. See you at lunch.'

He went to his studio to tidy up the previous day's mess. Screwed the caps on some tubes of paint that had leaked onto the table. Threw away a brush that was caked in dried paint. Cleaned another two with turpentine. Stared at a half-finished painting and examined the sketches strewn all over the floor. Then he picked up a brush and started to paint.

He tried to picture Puni, but could not. A veil seemed to descend over his eyes. He heard sounds, muffled then high pitched. It was as if the colours in the painting were speaking to him, as if they were people. They did not articulate words as such, rather chords and tones that represented different feelings. He worked fast, with zeal and energy.

The school bell rang for lunchtime, but he continued as if nothing had happened. Suddenly, someone appeared at the door. He saw a faint shadow moving in the glare of the wet paint on his canvas. He carried on, pretending he had not seen it. He knew who it was and he was not happy, which surprised him. She was interrupting him and he wanted to be alone.

'That's a really fantastic painting,' Puni said, stepping into the light streaming through the large studio windows.

He turned to look at her.

'So, do you want to come tonight?' she asked.

He giggled, uncertain.

'Wait one moment!' he said, and ran out into the corridor, down the stairs and into Tarique's studio on the floor below.

Tarique was sitting at his table, working on an illustration.

'Puni, from the first year, she wants to go out with me tonight...' PK started.

Tarique looked up.

'... So, should I go?' he continued breathlessly. 'She suggested going to the cinema.'

PK looked expectantly at his friend.

Tarique sighed.

'Jesus, Pradyumna, she's not going to kidnap you! Go have some fun!'

They waved down a motorcycle rickshaw and rode together to the cinema. They were going to see *Ajanabee*, a story about a middle-class boy who falls for a rich and beautiful upper-class girl. They sat down in the back on a cracked vinyl two-seater sofa. The dramatic opening music came blasting through the loudspeakers. It turned out to be a shocking tale. The girl fell pregnant but did not want to keep the child – how un-Indian, PK thought – because she wanted to become a model. The couple split and the girl moved back home to her father. The shame.

He liked the outdoor scenes, the singing and dancing. It was the most romantic movie on release at the time, that much he understood. He was lost in the spectacle until Puni wrenched him back to reality by reaching out and searching for his hand. Their fingers interlocked.

'My mother asked me where you keep all the money you earn from your art,' she whispered in his ear. 'If you want, she can take care of it for you.'

'No need, I opened a bank account,' he whispered back.

They sat in silence for a few minutes. The screen was alight with a passionate love scene. The hero kissed his girl, one of those typical Indian film kisses where everything is left to the imagination. Still, he squirmed with embarrassment, shook a little even. She squeezed his hand even harder.

'What's the matter?' she asked.

'Nothing,' he hissed back.

'But you're shaking.'

'It's cold. I'm cold.'

She leaned her head against his shoulder. 'No it's not.'

'Really?'

'I love you,' she said, and sighed heavily.

He felt confused, uneasy, weak even.

'I haven't... ever thought about love,' he faltered.

'Now you can,' she said.

'Well,' he tried again, 'according to the customs of my village, you can't fall in love unless you're married.'

The moustached leading man shot at a pickpocket who had just stolen his jewel-laden bag. The thief fell to the ground, dead.

'Oh, don't worry,' she said. 'Write a letter to your father and I will ask my parents. My mother likes you, she will convince my father. And then we can get married.'

She continued: 'You make a living from your art and I... well, I will also be an artist. We can be very happy together.'

He did not know what to say. All these dreams and plans. Maybe she was right? Maybe she was his future? Maybe he should write to his father and ask permission to get married? He was unsure how he really felt, but perhaps this was his fate. Everything happens for a reason.

Luckily, the ending of the film was a happy one, or he might have cried; with the couple reunited, the credits finally rolled.

They left the cinema hand in hand, hailed a rickshaw and rattled along the Vivekananda Road, glittering in the rain, towards Old Delhi. She jumped off near the Great Mosque and the rickshaw turned south towards his rented room in the suburbs.

Once home, he began to write a letter to his father. Puni's proposal sounded good, he thought, despite his somewhat conflicting emotions. She was right! She must have been the woman the astrologer meant. She certainly was not from his village or state. Not exactly from another country, but close enough.

A girl had fallen in love with him, he wrote, and they wanted to marry. Would his father give them permission?

He rubbed his eyes and looked at the clock. Half past midnight. He lay down on his bed, his thoughts spinning. A pack of wild dogs barked as they passed outside. The sound of a creaking bicycle came and disappeared. The rain had stopped and the window cast a milky white square of light on his dirty cement floor.

It had all been decided... And he drifted off to sleep.

The entrance hall to Puni's home was thick with the smell of spices; paratha, chicken curry, palak paneer, aloo ghobi. He was amazed to think that all this food had been prepared for him, that they had made such an effort for his sake. The dining room table was invisible under the sheer number of plates and bowls. There was no space left even for the napkins, which their servant girl had instead placed on a side table draped in a floral cloth.

He was starving.

'Namaste,' he said, placing his palms together as he bent down and touched her father's feet, a greeting he thought would satisfy any would-be father-in-law.

'Welcome, brother. Stand up,' Puni's father replied. 'We are modern people, let's shake hands instead.'

They were joined around the table by Puni's two brothers and their wives, while Puni sat in the next room behind a door covered by a curtain, where she could still hear their conversation.

This was how it was done, he knew that, but at the same time, it seemed absurd. He was here to be interviewed by her parents, not to see her.

But I'm supposed to be marrying Puni, not her father, he remembers thinking.

And her father's first question? 'What is your caste?'

PK felt his cheeks grow hot. This was not a good start. He knew the family belonged to a high caste. If they were traditional, there was no way he would be accepted as their son-in-law. Yet her father had just said they were modern people.

PK answered with a question. 'Do you believe in the caste system?' Full on counterattack was his only chance. Before Puni's father could answer, he continued: 'What does caste matter? I may have been born in a tribal region and my father may be untouchable, but the blood in my veins is still the same colour as your daughter's, is it not? We share the same interests. I hope we can be happy together.'

Puni's father looked him in the eye. No doors had yet been closed. A positive outcome was still within the realms of possibility.

'You were born in a tribal area to an untouchable family?'

PK did not answer this question.

'And my daughter is already in love with you?'

Everyone in the room fell silent. No one moved or made a sound, not even to clear their throat.

PK thought he heard her father's slow breathing and the sound of his own pulse. He looked around. All smiles were gone, faces flickered with uncertainty.

Finally, Puni's mother broke the silence. Or rather, the

sound of her hand slapping against her forehead did: 'Oh my God!'

Her father stood up, pointed at the door. 'Please leave my house!' he bellowed. 'Now! And never, *ever* contact my daughter again!'

PK stood up and walked out with barely a whispered goodbye.

Sobbing, he threw himself down on his bed. After the first violent convulsions of emotion had eased, he continued to lie there for some time, staring up at the ceiling. He was destroyed, empty and small. Memories of his school days in Athmallik came rushing back, the exclusion and rejection. That familiar feeling of inferiority had been secretly lying in wait, under the surface, demanding to be set free. His heart pounded, his skin burned, sweat drenched his body. He shook as if engulfed by fever.

He lay there for the rest of the night, his thoughts churning: Why, why, why was I born untouchable?

He saw her again a few days later, while he was drinking tea in the school café. She was talking to a male student. He approached but she turned away and left with the other man.

At lunch they ran into each other again. This time she made eye contact.

'Forget me!' she said quickly. She neither believed in, nor cared about, the caste system, but her father did, she explained. 'I cannot defy my father.'

He was dumbstruck.

'Did you see the guy I was talking to?' Puni said. 'He's reading engineering. My father had already arranged for us to marry, but he was prepared to change his mind because I told him that I was in love with you. But that was before he knew anything about your background.'

PK stared at her in amazement. She had pursued him so relentlessly, and yet within a few days, had agreed to marry someone else.

'It's over,' she said.

'Do you love him?' he asked.

'Yes,' she replied without moving a muscle in her face.

What kind of love was this? She's lying, PK thought. She's scared to defy her father.

'Puni, listen! I'll fight for us. Legally, no one can stop us. Not your father, not your family. We can get married without any of your relatives or a priest if need be, and then we can move to a place where no one can find us, where no one knows about us, or even cares.'

But she did not seem to be listening. She turned her head and her eyes flickered as she glanced down the corridor and into the canteen.

'Don't ever talk to me again,' she interrupted. 'Forget about me!'

'Don't you like me any more?'

'I like you, but I can't marry you.'

'Why not, Puni?'

'I can't make my father unhappy.'

PK had read in the newspapers about the Dalit Panthers from Bombay. Inspired by the Black Panthers in America, they had written a manifesto in which they claimed that Brahmin control of India was worse than British colonialism, just as his grandfather and father used to say. Hindu leaders held tight onto both the entire state apparatus and an inherited feudal power in the form of spiritual oppression, they wrote. 'We will not be easily satisfied now. We do not want a little place in the Brahmin alley,' their manifesto declared.

The untouchables had their own newspaper, *Dalit Voice*, in which the Dalit Panthers likened their discrimination to racism against blacks in the United States. African-Americans would never be free, they claimed, as long as their blood brothers and sisters in Asia were still suffering. Indeed, the Dalits were in an even more desperate situation, which could be compared to the height of slavery two hundred years earlier. PK was at home in his room in Lodi Colony, screaming at the walls:

'You Brahmins and the rest of you high-caste snobs! You prejudiced, stuck-up, narrow-minded creeps! What have we ever done to you?'

He could not sleep for all the hateful thoughts coursing through his head. He woke at four and lay in bed, wrestling with these voices, until the sun rose three hours later. Anger was followed by bitterness and self-pity.

A thin green book with yellowed paper, cloudy ink and slightly sloping text lay on his bedside table. He picked it up and began reading, to forget Puni.

One day, in Kerala, southern India, Shiva
decided to teach the Brahmins a lesson.

Ah, this is perfect, PK thought, and continued reading.

Shiva, the book said, wanted to put a stop to the overblown pride of the Kerala Brahmins and decided to humiliate the highest and brightest of them all, the exalted spiritual teacher Adi Shankaracharya.

The guru was close to enlightenment. The only thing preventing Adi from being freed from the cycle of rebirth was his own arrogance and pride, his refusal to accept that he was of the same flesh and blood as all other humans on Earth, no matter what caste or social position.

Shiva and his wife Parvati wanted to play a trick on him. They transformed into a poor, lowly couple of the untouchable Pulayar caste. Their son Nandikesan joined them, turning himself into their wretched child. They were dressed as day labourers, their clothes smeared with dirt from the fields. In addition, Shiva conjured up the smells of meat and alcohol, taboos for virtuous Brahmins. Shiva reeked as if he had been drinking all night. Just to reinforce his point, he carried a jug of palm wine under one arm and had a half coconut shell of the pungent liquor in the other.

And so, on one of the raised paths through the paddies, Shiva, Parvati and their son encountered Adi Shankaracharya. Custom dictated that an untouchable should jump down from the embankment and into the mud when faced with a Brahmin. But Shiva and his family kept walking straight towards Adi and asked *him* to step aside so that they might pass.

The arrogant Adi was enraged.

'How dare a family like you, dirty, smelly, drunk, meat-eating untouchables, walk on the same path as a pure and unblemished Brahmin? You smell like you haven't washed once in your lives. I've never seen anything like it,' Adi thundered, and threatened to behead them, on the grounds that this was a crime that even the gods would never forgive.

Shiva replied: 'I admit, I have partaken of a glass or two, and it was a while since I last bathed. But before I climb down into this muddy field, I want you to explain to me what makes you, a clean and high-caste Brahmin, different to us dirty untouchables. Let me ask you a few questions.'

If Adi was able to answer them, Shiva promised he and his family would let him pass as propriety dictated.

'My first question,' Shiva began. 'If we both cut our hands, is not our blood the same colour? My second question: Do we not eat rice from the same field? My third question: Do you not give bananas, grown by the untouchables, as offerings to the gods? My fourth question: Do you not adorn the gods with flowers picked by our women?

My fifth question: Do we not dig the wells that provide the water you use in your temple rituals?'

Adi could not answer Shiva's questions, so continued:

'Just because you eat on metal plates and we on banana leaves does not mean that we belong to different species. You Brahmins ride elephants and we buffaloes, but that does not make you elephants and us buffaloes.'

Adi was not only dumbfounded by the wretched man's words, they confused him. How could this poor, illiterate untouchable, who had hardly any schooling, come up with such sophisticated and profound philosophical questions? So Adi began to meditate right there on the path and opened his sixth sense. At once he understood: the dirty Pulayar family faded and in their place appeared the gods, Shiva, Parvati and their son Nandikesan, in all their splendour.

Horrified by what he had done, Adi fell to his knees and recited a poem in honour of Shiva.

Shiva forgave him.

Adi asked him why he had turned himself into an untouchable when he appeared to him, his most devoted follower.

'Yes, you are a wise man on your way to salvation and enlightenment,' replied Shiva. 'But you will never get there unless you understand that all people deserve respect and empathy. I took this form to teach you this. You must fight against prejudice and ignorance and help people from all castes, not just your fellow Brahmins. Only then will you achieve true enlightenment.'

Thousands of years ago, Shiva had taught the Brahmin a lesson. And yet here was PK, all these years later, the poor untouchable still drawing comfort from Shiva's story.

There was hope, he realized. In Kerala, where Shiva is particularly celebrated to this day, many people saw an heir to this story in the doctrines of Karl Marx. PK understood in that moment that God was not merely a tool for oppressing the poor, but also a shield against the arrogance of the privileged, a potential catalyst to effect change in the world.

PK went to see a psychologist, who told him in no uncertain terms that he was not to mope around at home alone in Lodi Colony, but rather he should get out and socialize.

'Try to enjoy life,' he said encouragingly.

PK consulted a friend at school, who told him to try alcohol. It had given his friend solace after the particularly painful end to a love affair.

'It helped,' he said.

PK had never let a drop pass his lips before, indeed the idea had never occurred to him. Alcohol was for the weak-willed. But feeling desperate, he went to one of the shops in the backstreets behind Connaught Place and bought a small bottle of Indian-made foreign liquor. He found a spot in the shade, hidden behind a load of mattresses. He poured half the bottle down his throat, hissed, coughed and spat out what remained in his mouth. Then he sat down on some steps and waited. And waited. But he felt nothing.

After some time, his surroundings began to feel soft, like cotton wool. It was a nice feeling, as if the pain and grief of recent weeks were floating away. His friend was right: alcohol helped.

He went to the fountain to work but could barely hold a pencil. He apologized – he was sick, he said – packed up his stuff and hobbled home. He slept the rest of the evening and through the night, only to wake up late the next morning and reach immediately for what remained of the bottle of whisky.

He drank more and more. For the next few weeks, alcohol was the first thing he tasted in the morning and the last thing at night. It made him feel like someone, or rather something, cared for him. The hard edges of the world were wrapped in a gossamer mist. Corners became round and worries faded.

Wobbling up Parliament Street with a sketchbook under his arm, he ran into one of the policemen he had drawn in the past. The officer could smell the booze on his breath and was blunt in his greeting: 'Why have you started drinking?'

PK started to tell his story. He told him all about Puni, the trip to the cinema, how he had been shaken by love, the invitation to meet her parents, all the food they had made for his visit, her father, his banishment, the humiliation and his fear that no one would ever love an untouchable like him. He stank of whisky and his monologue was loud and energetic. He had difficulty keeping his balance, swaying back and forth like a mast in the wind. Then he cried.

The officer stood and listened patiently without interrupting him, except to ask him to repeat the parts he could not catch through PK's mumbling and slurring.

The further he got into the story, the better PK started to feel.

'Oh, don't be stupid,' the policeman said finally. 'May I see your hand?'

PK held it out. The officer studied the lines on his palm.

'Look here, it will all be fine! According to these lines, you will marry suddenly and unexpectedly, and the marriage will be a wonderful and happy one.'

'But,' PK continued in his garbled speech, 'I'm untouchable. I'll never be able to marry a Hindu woman, at least not one who can read and write and comes from a decent family.'

'Maybe she won't be Indian,' came the policeman's simple reply.

That night, as he lay in bed navigating the borderland between wakefulness and sleep, bitter memories ambushed him. He was eternally doomed and yet also fated to something better.

She came to him in his dream, an angel in white. She had travelled across the wheatfields of the Punjab and over New Delhi's rooftops, and landed here, in his room. They were so close now they could touch each other.

He drank in her presence, her breath, her scent and her soft hair as it fluttered against his bare shoulders. He felt her warmth and affection and somehow knew things his conscious mind did not. She was somehow bigger than him, not physically, but spiritually.

He awoke, but she felt more like vapour, faceless and cold. And yet, her presence lingered with him into his waking hours.

She returned the following night. This time she came with melodies he had never heard before. It's beautiful over there, he thought. Just like the fortune teller said.

It was the spring of 1975, and violent demonstrations had broken out against rising food prices and the internal bickering of Hindu nationalists. Discontent was reaching boiling point.

Even Indira Gandhi was unhappy. She was angry with antagonistic judges, critical journalists and quarrelling opposition politicians who she believed did not have the necessary skills to take responsibility for the country. What infuriated her most, however, was that she stood accused of electoral fraud. A court ruled that she had bribed voters in the last election and, contrary to the law, spent government money on her own personal election campaign. She was stripped of her seat in Parliament and forbidden to stand again for six years.

But Indira was not going to stand idly by and watch as her opponents moved against her. She took matters into her own hands and, on 25 June, she asked the President to issue a state of emergency, citing 'internal disturbance' as the justification. In this one move, she had annulled the court's decision to limit her powers and instead grabbed hold of the reins of government herself. Early the next morning, while the first monsoon rains of the season fell across New Delhi, she gathered together her ministers to tell them what was happening, and then took to the airwaves to inform the people.

'There's no reason to panic,' her voice sounded in millions of crackling radios as clouds clogged the sky above.

From then on, she was the sole person in charge. Indira was India, and India was Indira, as the Congress Party spokesman told the press.

But before her speech was broadcast to the people, politicians and government officials had already whispered the news to the sleepy chai boys on Parliament Road, to the Sikh taxi drivers parked under the trees of Patel Chowk, and to the itinerant sugar-cane vendors in Tolstoy Marg. Like fire through the forest, word engulfed the city's colonial arcades, spread among the bus drivers who goaded their crowded vehicles along Radial Road No. 1, and to the waiters at the Indian Coffee House, who served it to their guests alongside their hot drinks. Within five minutes, everyone in the city already knew what Indira was about to say.

In the aftermath, the press was censored, opposition politicians were imprisoned, and trade unions subjugated. Journalists and intellectuals criticized the Prime Minister. But Indira was convinced that the landless and the oppressed supported her, that PK and his brothers and sisters, India's millions and millions of poor, stood by her side.

It was their backing she had to win if she was to remain in power. And PK believed she would bring order to the country. Leaders who looked after the poor had justice on their side.

Delhi was papered with Maoist-sounding slogans. As he walked his usual route to the fountain at Connaught Place, posters screamed out at him:

COURAGE AND CLEAR VISION – YOUR NAME IS INDIRA GANDHI

A SMALL FAMILY IS A HAPPY FAMILY

WORK MORE, TALK LESS

EFFICIENCY IS OUR CRY

And the one that sounded like an advertisement for the Indian Coffee House:

Be Indian, Buy Indian

Otherwise, it was mostly business as usual.

The country's most prominent businessman, Mr JRD Tata, claimed that the strikes, boycotts and demonstrations had gone too far. The parliamentary system had not adapted to the country's needs.

The middle classes, shopkeepers, businessmen and government officials said they were tired of the chaos, and that they preferred the police to receive new powers that would allow them to disperse threatening crowds by force if necessary, to lock up the petty thieves and ensure that the slums that had grown up along Delhi's avenues were demolished. In the Indian Coffee House, PK heard comments like:

'Opposition politicians, intellectuals and journalists just complain about the state of emergency. But we ordinary people, we like it.'

And:

'Delhi needs a strong hand. The slums are everywhere these days.'

Even:

'Now, crime has fallen, the trains run on time, the streets are cleaned and people are sterilized so that we don't have ten children in every slum shack. But the newspapers only complain about human rights violations and rubbish like that. Things are finally improving.'

But Delhi's teachers, journalists and academics were shocked and angry.

'How could she? It's her son Sanjay who's behind it, the punk. And the President? He's nothing but a joke, Indira's stooge.'

Raids took place around the capital and prominent politicians, lawyers and newspaper editors, who Indira now saw as enemies of the state, were arrested. People resigned in response. The protests began to tail off. But a minority persevered and continued to demonstrate in the streets against 'Indira's madness', as their placards called it.

Once a month, the Sikh People's Front for Civil Rights organized protest marches on the streets of Delhi. PK heard how they roared their slogans as they passed the café. He went outside to watch. The procession of men dressed in traditional ankle-length robes and blue and orange turbans floated down the avenue towards Parliament.

'Indira is mad and so is India!' the leader chanted.

The city was boiling over, that much was obvious, but the newspapers gave the impression that all was calm and peaceful. Not a word was printed about the protests.

Opposition to Indira became increasingly inventive, coming up with methods to fool the censors. A post in the obituary section of *The Times of India* reported the anonymous contributor's regret at the tragic death of *D. E. M. O'Cracy*, survived by his mourning wife, *T. Ruth*, his son *L. I. Bertie* and his daughters *Faith*, *Hope* and *Justice*.

How gullible can the censors be? PK laughed to himself.

PK liked Indira, but the state of emergency was too much, even for him. He was forced to report to Haksar that some police officers were becoming more aggressive in their methods. They chased people away from his queue, ripped up his paintings and shouted at him to leave. It was as if one half of the force did not know what the other was doing. One day he was met with friendly concern, the next with a stinging slap. Their treatment of him was inconsistent to say the least.

Haksar listened silently and then told PK he would make some calls. He assured him that he would ensure the police left him alone.

The next day, Delhi's governor arrived at the fountain in his official car, his advisers and servants in tow. Police harassment would cease immediately, he reported. Henceforth, no officer of the law would be allowed to arrest him because he used a public place as his private gallery.

A few days after the governor's visit, men from the State Electricity Board arrived to install lighting so that he would be able to work late into the evenings. He was also assigned a personal assistant, a man who would run his errands, buy food, drinks, pens and paper, as well as pack up and lock away his paintings in a specially arranged store when he finished for the night.

'Anything else I can help with, sir?' his assistant said with a salute as he closed the store.

Haksar explained that the area around the fountain was going to become New Delhi's Montmartre. Just like the Place du Tertre in Paris, artists would be allowed to work freely. PK would become a tourist attraction.

The Statesman published an article a few days before Christmas 1975 about PK and the other artists around the fountain. *Your face is his fortune*, it declared. Just as in Paris, portraits were the mainstay of their business, rather than the more thoroughly considered works, the newspaper noted.

> It takes ten minutes and ditto rupees to get a pencil likeness of yourself from Pradyumna Kumar Mahanandia... One among the seven artists holding their exhibitions in the basement of Delhi's Connaught Place Fountain, PK has been the most successful. He earns anything between Rs 40 and Rs 150 every evening sketching passers-by and visitors to the exhibition.

> 'Few people want to invest money in a landscape or on a modern art painting, but no

one minds spending just Rs 10 for a portrait of theirs – especially if it's done in ten minutes,' observes Jagdish Chandra Sharma, one of the other exhibiting artists.

After an unprofitable month exhibiting paintings that never got sold, Jagdish took a leaf out of PK's art book and started making portraits. And soon his pockets too were jingling.

PK lay on his bed, reading about Robert Clive, a strange Englishman who after his death became known as Clive of India. PK was fascinated by the story, and recognized himself in the foreign man's unwillingness to give in to his father's expectations, in his yearning for adventure and even his unsuccessful suicide attempts. He could have been reading about himself.

Robert Clive was a disappointment to his father. He was born in 1725, the most rebellious of thirteen children, hyperactive, stubborn and insubordinate. He was deemed so unruly by the age of three that he was sent away from the family estate to be taken care of by childless relatives in town. But they were unable to cope, and he was sent back to the village after a few years.

At the age of ten, he used to climb up the clock tower in a devil mask and scare passers-by below. By his teens, he was a petty criminal. Exhausted, his father eventually found him a job – on the other side of the world. He was to work as a bookkeeper at the East India Company's offices in Madras. The family were relieved to be rid of him. It was well known that the odds of returning from India were only about fifty-fifty: he was just as likely to die from some tropical illness as make it back to the shores of Great

Britain. But the eighteen-year-old Robert Clive was happy to be finally embarking on his own adventure.

The job in Madras turned out to be deathly boring, however, and suffering insomnia, anxiety and depression, he put a gun to his temple and pulled the trigger. *Click!* He tried again. *Click! Click!*

PK could not put the book down.

Everything happened for a reason, Clive concluded. God must have had a greater plan for him.

Just like me, PK thought. It was all decided at birth.

Robert Clive established the East India Company as a powerful military and political entity, helping to lay the foundations of the British Raj that allowed the British Empire to flourish.

After returning to England, Clive was honoured with the title of Baron. Yet he spent his last years fighting to clear his name after being accused of misconduct. Despite eventual success, he committed suicide in 1773. His fellow countrymen were reminded of his story every time they visited the Tower of London museum, where his elephant had been stuffed and put on display in its armour. Who knows, perhaps it was one of PK's ancestors who had captured that very animal, and tamed it for the local king, who had then sold it on to the Englishman?

PK closed the book. Robert Clive had played a part in securing India for the British, and had even been posted to Orissa. Had it not been for him, perhaps India would have become French. Or remained under the rule of the Muslim kings or Hindu autocrats. PK's family said that British victory had been the best of all possible outcomes, for untouchables like them at least.

He read in *The Times of India* about another book, this time about two famous Englishmen who visited the jungle he grew up in.

According to the article, the book was almost one hundred years old. He saw in the picture the gilt lettering embossed on a brown leather cover, with two long stalks of grass, a coat of arms and two crossed spears: *Jungle Life in India*. The author, an Irishman by the name of Valentine Ball, called himself a geologist and ornithologist and had spent almost twenty years travelling around India, documenting everything from the stones he found at the bottom of rivers, to rocks scattered in the dirt and birds nesting in the treetops. But the thing that caught PK's eye was that he had lived many years in Orissa, wandering through the same jungle that PK had played in as a child and along the very river he washed in with his mother.

He put the newspaper down. A strong smell of burning leaves came wafting in through the open window, probably from the evening fire the neighbourhood street sweeper made to keep himself warm in the chilly winter night. Beeping scooters and barking dogs provided the bedtime lullaby.

But it was still too early to sleep. His head was full of all the Europeans who had visited his homeland. Wide awake, he picked up his copy of Rudyard Kipling's *The Jungle Book*. It was odd that a white-skinned English gentleman would write a story about an Indian boy raised by wolves. The same story that Grandma, who had never heard of Kipling's book, used to tell him as he rolled around on his straw mat before bed. He knew by heart the story of the boy who lived with wolves. His grandma had even begun varying the storyline, expanding it with new details and plot twists in an effort not to bore her grandson, or herself. It was a widely known myth of the jungle in India, long before Kipling was even born.

PK only learned that the Englishman had written a book based on the story when he got to school. He read the protagonist's name again and again to himself:

'Mowgli, Mowgli, Mowgli...'

Why did Kipling name him that? Monguli, as it was pronounced in Oriya, was a common boy's name where he came from, but barely heard elsewhere in India. Kipling claimed the book was inspired by the Pench National Park in the neighbouring state of Madhya Pradesh, but his choice of name for his protagonist suggested that Kipling had also visited PK's forest.

His grandfather and Bapa used to talk about an English author who lived for some time in the State Forest Agency guesthouse in Kansab Kurab, a few hours' walk north of the shores of the Mahanadi River. Which meant Kipling must have read Valentine Balls's *Jungle Life in India* and come to Athmallik himself, heard the name and given it to his main character, albeit with a new spelling.

Kipling wrote that Mowgli meant frog in the language of the forest. Mother and Father Wolf chose the name because Mowgli had smooth skin with no fur and never sat still. But there was no forest language in real life. And why would parents give their child a name that means frog? In Oriya, Monguli described the dawn and meant light, hope and optimism.

But the story was fading, along with his childhood and the forest, and his thoughts turned back to 1975. The imprisonments, the censorship and the sinking morale, they would all be temporary, that was what PK had thought at the time. The darkness wouldn't be permanent either, not for India and not for him. Indira Gandhi would release her iron grip. One day, the untouchables would be free and he would meet the woman from his prophecy.

'I'm going to India. I've decided. It's my mission in life,' Lotta told her parents.

They did not object. Lotta had expected opposition, but they remained calm and told her she knew best, as if she had announced that she was taking the bus to Gothenburg. Neither said much in general, anyway. They were used to it, she thought. She was only twenty but had already spent a year living abroad on her own in the UK. Moreover, she knew they too had dreamed of travelling the world but circumstances had prevented it.

They would have done the same in my situation, she thought.

There was no heroism in her plans. Lotta was not doing it for the spectacle, to break records. She was not writing an adventure story. There were no boats between Europe and India and flying cost a fortune, so that was out of the question. The train went as far as Mashhad in eastern Iran, but after that the plains gave way to mountains through which no train could travel, all through Afghanistan up to the border with Pakistan. No, the train was too complicated. There were regular bus services all the way from London to New Delhi and Kathmandu. One company, calling itself the Magic Bus, had already become an icon of the hippy era, with its colourfully painted coaches and dirt cheap prices.

Lotta considered her options, but really, she had already decided. Driving was the only sensible option. She had a licence, and companions: Leif, an ex-boyfriend of her sister, and her best friend, with her Indian husband and their baby. They would drive to Gothenburg, take the ferry to Kiel, proceed along the autobahn to the Alps, continue over the Balkans and then roll into Istanbul, the gateway to the East.

As for the specifics, they'd work them out along the way. They had maps but no guidebooks, for the simple reason that no guidebooks yet existed for the route. And why plan a trip that would keep changing? The journey was to be like life itself, unpredictable and exciting.

They bought a green 1971 VW van with help from Lotta's father. The vehicle had already done one round trip to Iran and back after which the engine gave up in exhaustion, but it had since been replaced. Newly serviced, the van was as good as ready, if not new.

Her mother offered only one piece of advice: 'Behave in such a way that you can always feel proud of yourself. And never do any harm to anyone else.'

It was October 1975. Lotta sat behind the wheel of their hippy dream and drove out into the world. There was no waving, no big goodbye, no fanfares sounding in the streets of Borås. But the adventure had begun.

It was a cold December evening. The coloured lights had been switched on and shone in patterns on the water's surface. For once, there was no queue of waiting customers and no crowd of curious onlookers watching as he drew. PK was done for the night anyway, so he began taking down his paintings from the cardboard sheets on which they were displayed.

Out of the darkness, a young European woman appeared and asked if he would be at the fountain the next day. She wore a yellow T-shirt and tight, flared jeans. He noticed that she did not wear make-up. She seemed different from the other European women he usually talked to at the Indian Coffee House, more serious and thoughtful. But she was in a hurry. He answered her, and she gave only a quick 'thank you' before disappearing into the night.

Was she afraid of me? Would she come back?

The next afternoon, he took his place by the fountain earlier than usual. He was hoping to meet the serious white woman again and had therefore put on his new jeans with their snaking yellow stitching on the back pockets, and the short-sleeved green checked shirt that his neighbour Didi had so kindly ironed for him. He had trimmed his moustache that morning to reveal his upper lip and combed his hair with coconut oil to tame the unruly curls. The tourists were already waiting for him. As he and his helper unpacked the canvases and began rigging up the easel, a queue formed. He looked around for the unadorned woman with the sober face. But she was nowhere to be seen.

At nine o'clock he gave up his wait, packed away his equipment and walked home to Lodi Colony. The disappointment wore heavily on him.

She had specifically asked him if he would be there, why

then had she not come? He had already woven together a full fantasy out of their minute-long meeting. At home, sitting on his bed, he began to pray, listing all the names of the gods he could think of, not only from the Hindu pantheon, but Allah, Buddha, Mahavira, the Dalai Lama, the Christian God and Maharishi Mahesh Yogi. There, in his dingy room, he prayed to them all, every god, guru and prophet his memory could conjure into existence.

The next day, a thick winter fog enveloped the city, as was usual for this time of year. He decided to go to the Shiva temple to pray that the woman with the soft voice would come back. He appealed to the Auspicious One for a full hour. He had never done that before. Normally, he did not go in for religious entreaties. But this time, he was desperate.

At home in Athmallik, he was forbidden from even entering the temple. But here in New Delhi, people from different castes, classes and ethnic groups gathered as if it were the most normal thing in the world. No one kept watch nor cared about caste. The anonymity and diversity of the big city gave him at least a partial sense of his longed for freedom.

After the temple, he made his way to Connaught Place. The columns and pilasters of the Romanesque buildings stood like mysterious figures in a dream. Just before dusk, the pale winter sun broke through the mist. There were even more people today. Some sat on the grass as they had their ears cleaned by men with dirty cotton buds. Others lay on their stomachs as men kneaded their muscles with their feet. But most sat or reclined in groups, content to chat, shell peanuts, smoke, and chew on paan, spitting out the blood red juices where they sat. Today, perhaps, she would come.

Her mother had always wanted pencil drawings of her daughters, Lotta recalled as she stood by the fountain on Connaught Place. *Ten rupees, ten minutes*, the sign said.

The queue was usually long, but that evening, she caught sight of the street artist in a rare moment of solitude, gazing at the cascading water. She stepped out of the shadows and asked him a question. What it was, she can no longer recall, but the conversation was brief. She then said goodbye and quickly left. There was something about him that both attracted and frightened her, and she decided she could always return the next day to have her portrait done.

Two nights later, she was back in the queue by the fountain. When it was her turn, she told him she wanted a portrait in pencil. He stared at her, as if it was a remarkable request. She examined his moustache and the frizz on the top of his head that he was obviously trying to tame with a slick of grease. He flipped to a fresh piece of paper and prepared himself. His hair glistened under the streetlamps. A darker version of Jimi Hendrix, she thought. He was clearly copying the hippy style. And yet he also looked like the curly-haired forest boy from Elsa Beskow's picture book, *Bubble Muck*, who lived among the lily pads and presented a fairy with a shiny ring.

It was just after seven on the evening of 17 December 1975, and the smog-filled sky over Delhi shimmered a peach colour in the glow of the streetlights. This was to be the first time they really saw each other.

A throng of people had gathered around the fountain as usual, but he saw her, there in the crowd. Her long, blonde hair. Finally! She was waiting in the queue. When her turn came, he told her to sit down on the stool. His hand was shaking as he traced his pencil over the paper. An audience stood around him as always, but he was used to them; they were not the ones making him nervous.

His marks were so unsteady that he had to give up.

'I'm sorry, I can't draw,' he said. 'Would you be willing to come to the art school tomorrow instead?'

'Sure, we'll come,' she said.

He looked up. A white man was waiting behind her. Her husband? Please no.

'Yes, both of you,' he said cheerily.

'My name is Lotta, this is Leif. He's a photographer.'

She didn't say boyfriend, or husband, he thought hopefully.

He showered, put on some clean clothes, examined himself in the mirror and said her name to himself again. At first he thought she had said Lata, which was the name of the singer whose songs he heard all the time in the movies.

No. She said Lotta.

His neighbour Didi came out onto her veranda.

'Are you going for a job interview?' she asked.

'In a way,' he replied.

When he arrived at the school he fetched three wooden chairs, placed them in the sun on the lawn outside the café, and sat down to wait. They arrived at ten on the dot, as agreed. Yes please, to coffee.

It was a nice feeling, to sit in the clear December air with a cup of steaming coffee in his hands, opposite these two new friends. He had not yet asked where they were from.

'Sweden,' she said suddenly, as if she had read his thoughts. 'We come from Sweden.'

'Far away,' he said.

They nodded.

'In Europe,' he added. A guess.

She smiled.

'Come, let me show you the school,' he said, when they had finished their coffee.

Leif stopped to talk to some students in the ground floor corridor, while PK and Lotta went around on their own. He introduced her to his teachers and showed her the lecture halls and studios that occupied the seven-storey building. It was as if she was an old friend, he thought, even though they had only known each other for half an hour.

After they had examined every nook and cranny of the building, he asked her what she liked most in life.

'Music,' she replied. 'I play the flute.'

He asked her star sign.

'Taurus,' she said.

She will be born in the sign of Taurus and be musical...

He gathered his courage, and asked politely: 'Is Leif your husband?'

'What?'

He had mumbled, spoken too quickly, fearing it would sound ridiculous. Had she not heard him? Was she offended? Maybe one should not ask such questions of a woman? He repeated his question.

'No,' she laughed. 'Leif? We're not married. And he's not my boyfriend either.'

They continued their tour. The other students whispered to each other and pointed as he walked beside the foreign woman. Even Puni, who had not so much as looked in his direction in recent months, came up and said hello. He enjoyed the feeling, letting her see him with Lotta.

He asked if Lotta and Leif wanted to come to his room in

Lodi Colony. 'Not that there's much to see really,' he added, but he was keen to show her his prints and oil paintings. She accepted the invitation without much enthusiasm.

Maybe she was just shy?

His room was as desolate and dirty as it had ever been. Lotta and Leif stood behind him on the veranda as he gazed inside. It was a sad sight. A broken cup had been thrown into a corner. The room was almost empty of furniture. He had not wiped the table. The floor was covered in gravel. Dust bunnies had collected by the back door and the walls were plastered with charcoal drawings and scrawls that he had made while drunk. One read: *I was born untouchable. I have no right to anything, not even love.* But most embarrassing of all: *I will marry a European girl as the astrologers have predicted.* He blocked their entrance, but it was no use. They had come to see how he lived, and he had to let them in.

He selected some prints and gave them to Lotta. She said nothing.

Had she read what he had written on the walls?

Then she smiled at him and thanked him for the gift.

She agreed to see him again, and the next day they met at Connaught Place to do a tour of the city on a motor rickshaw. They visited the great Jama Masjid mosque and listened to the call to prayer.

'It was built by a powerful man called Shah Jahan, Ruler of the World,' he told her and slowly repeated the call: '*La Allah illah Allah, Mohammad Resul-allah,*' he said, stressing every syllable, before translating, 'There is no god but God, and Mohammed is his prophet.'

They climbed to the top of one of the mosque's minarets and looked out over the people below and the Red Fort. From there, he told her, the Mughals, Persians and Britons had all ruled. They looked the other way to the

Gate of India, the main boulevard of the Republic and the Presidential Palace.

'It's amazing,' he said quietly.

'What's amazing?' asked Lotta.

'You see over there, the red bridge? That's called Minto Bridge. I used to sleep under it. I have spent nights cold and hungry there. And over there...' – he raised his hand slightly and pointed at the Presidential Palace a few kilometres further in the distance – 'the President of India invited me to tea.'

She searched across the cluttered landscape of Delhi until eventually she found the large dome.

'It's like a fairytale,' she said, but looked somewhat sceptical. Maybe she thought he was making it up?

They jumped into a rickshaw and headed south to Humayan's Tomb, one of the city's top tourist attractions. They chatted the whole way. It was so easy to talk to her. He thought again about the prophecy: she would be musical and born under the sign of Taurus.

And would own a jungle, the astrologer had added.

She could not possibly own a jungle, surely?

Lotta carried on with her travels. The next day, she and her friends took the VW bus for a trip out of the city. They headed for the temples of Khajuraho by the Ganges, where they could drink in the sight of pilgrims bathing in the holy water at Varanasi. PK missed her, but he had doubts. She was a tourist, she would soon be leaving India again. Life had so much to offer her, there was no way she would stay with him. Why would she? One moment. An eternity. His misgivings mixed with the memory of her gentle voice.

On Christmas Day, his birthday, he received a hand-pressed envelope with his name and address written on it in neat block capitals. He opened it with a pounding heart. He removed the colourful card with a drawing of a happy fish jumping out of clumsily drawn waves. Vulgar, his teachers would have said. Commercial. Infantile. But he had never received a birthday card before. He held it up to the sun so that the fish glowed.

> Imagine, we had to travel so far to find a nice friend like you. Happy birthday,

> Lotta.

The days before her return were sweet torment.

He caught sight of Leif and his large backpack in the rust-red dusk of New Year's Eve. PK ran through the crowds gathered around the fountain. Leif was alone and proceeded to tell PK about their trip to Khajuraho and the thousand-year-old temples with their erotic sculptures. Did PK know of a good, cheap hotel?

'Don't stay in a hotel, stay with me.'

He gave him the key to his room in Lodi Colony.

'What about Lotta?' PK ventured.

'She's renting a room in a palace. We met the family on the train.'

'She'd also be welcome at mine,' he said listlessly.

He had no hope that she would exchange a bed in a private room in the plush villa of a wealthy family for his cramped and filthy quarters.

The next day, as he sat gazing out along the street, a yellow-red dot appeared in the shade of the trees. It began to grow, slowly transforming into the contours of a woman. She was wearing jeans, a yellow T-shirt and a red backpack.

It felt like a personal triumph. He wanted to shout out in glee: she chose my poverty above their luxury!

But his greeting was more neutral, more controlled: 'Welcome, Lotta!'

Leif slept in PK's broken *charpoy*, a wooden bed with a braided rope base. For Lotta, he rolled out a thin bamboo mattress. He slept directly on the cement floor.

'Don't worry, I'm used to sleeping on hard ground,' he reassured them.

What bothered him most was that he had no linen to offer. But she looked happy enough as she rolled out her sleeping bag on the bamboo mat under the window.

He prepared masala omelette, toast and tea on a gas stove on the veranda. Then they took a motor rickshaw to Connaught Place, where they switched to a pat-pattie, a three-wheeled motorcycle overloaded with passengers, and headed for Old Delhi.

The city, of which he had been so afraid three years earlier, was now a part of him. She has to experience the markets, he said to himself. They are the reason I am the man I am today.

They wandered around the old town and through a narrow opening, wedged between two small restaurants, into an alley that swelled to form a small courtyard lit by fluorescent lights.

It smelled of charcoal and fried meat; plumes of steam rose from the outdoor kitchen, and diners sat at tables in the four different rooms around the courtyard. They peered inside one of them: there were floor-to-ceiling tiles and guests eating kebabs and thin, floury bread.

They walked around the groves and man-made lakes of Delhi Zoo housed in a dilapidated fort, talking and laughing. He felt giddy. And yet, anxiety began to ripple inside him as soon as they sat down on the lawn. He was waiting for tragedy to strike; his luck always ran out at some point. That was his experience of life so far, and it was how it would be now. Happiness was merely the premonition of impending misfortune. He was not created for true happiness. Lotta would travel back to Europe, and he would remain in India. She had come like a flash of lightning and would disappear again just as suddenly.

He had one semester left at the College of Art, and no money for travel.

It's impossible, he thought, our romance has no future, our meeting is doomed to be a short but pleasant memory and nothing more.

But he did not share these feelings with Lotta.

They continued on to Paharganj, Delhi's main market. They pressed tight against each other as they wove between fruit stalls and teashops. He felt at once consumed by her and by the pleasure of that moment. They talked with baker boys who flattened lumps of dough in red-hot tandoori ovens using only their hands. They met the bloodshot eyes of old men and women who lay outside on their charpoys, wrapped in grey sheets. They nearly tripped over a man who had dismantled a gearbox and had laid out the pieces, down to the washers, in a neat pattern on a piece of cardboard in the middle of the road. They picked their way through a herd of goats. They patted the shiny skins of cows, smelled the warm wet fabric of a woman ironing shirts with a steam iron. They laughed at the man who whipped milk with a converted electric drill. And they stood for several minutes watching an old man building a pyramid out of hundreds of chicken eggs under a naked light bulb. 'If one falls, they all go,' the egg man said. They laughed.

They saw dogs sashaying through the crowds, women sewing, silver necklaces being repaired, a girl who swept the street before her door. They breathed in smoke heavy with the smell of burnt leaves and listened as a woman snored. People sang, talked, rolled dough, played cards, and reclined in the shade.

He felt as if they were part of it all, the people and the streets, the smells and the sky.

* * *

They arrived at the fountain at around six o'clock, and PK started hanging out his paintings. Lotta helped him. He watched as she hooked them onto the cardboard screens. God, let this woman be my future wife, he thought, as he sat down on his stool. He then began working on the queue of people waiting. She sat close to him. He finished four drawings before they decided to pack up and go to the cinema instead.

Hundreds of people stood outside the Plaza. The queue for the box office snaked out into the street. *Sholay* had had its premiere six months previously, but it still drew full houses. They stood and looked at the hand-painted posters of Amitabh Bachchan pumping the bad guys full of lead from his machine gun. Once inside, they looked down on the stalls from their seats in the balcony and saw that most of the audience was made up of single men, gazing longingly back at them.

The movie started and he translated for her. But he paused when Lata Mangeshkar began to sing 'Jab Tak Hai Jaan', leaned back and just listened. Lotta moved closer to him during the film's more colourful dances, rested her head against his shoulder and put her hand in his. The fear, which he had been keeping at bay since leaving the zoo, returned with force. What did it all mean? Was there a higher power trying to tell him something? Was this how love began? He knew nothing and realized just how inexperienced he really was. He felt twelve years old again.

What will be will be. He had to overcome his misgivings. We have already started a new togetherness, he said to himself. Our souls are on the same wavelength.

He leaned forward and kissed her forehead.

'*Maheswari Ma, Ma Maheswari*', he whispered. A prayer to the same jungle goddess his mother used to call on in times of need.

It was winter in Delhi. The night sky was filled with stars but the fog held off until just before dawn. The air was ice-cold as they trudged through the deserted city past the fountain, which looked empty and desolate in the darkness. They walked along the main avenue south, past Raj Path and the triumphal India Gate, towards Lodi Colony. At first he held her hand, but as they were alone, he gathered his courage and put his arm around her. He felt the warmth of her body, but was also assailed by the feeling that he was doing something forbidden, that the streetlights were watching them. For a moment, he thought he had left his own body and was looking down, watching himself walking, side by side, with Lotta.

It was a long way home. But what of it? They arrived back at two in the morning. Leif was asleep in the rope bed, snoring loudly. They took a blanket and went out onto the veranda. They sat on the cement stairs and wrapped themselves up against the cold. Wild dogs yapped as they ran past. He held her, looked up at the stars, then at her and then up at the stars again. It was so romantic. And yet he was too shy to look straight into her eyes. The sky above was his escape.

They had been drawn together by a divine power, a power that had been working on him ever since he was born. He knew Westerners did not think like this. But that was how he had been brought up, that was how life worked. This was their night, their magic, their love, and it had been written in the stars. He kissed her again on the forehead, then on the cheeks. First the eyes, then the mind, and then the heart, love made its way through him. They had always belonged together, and together they would stay, for time in all its infinity.

He whispered her name. She did not answer. So they remained in silence.

'I love you,' he ventured. But instantly, he regretted it.

Why? Why did those words, of all the ones he could have chosen, have to leap out of his mouth? What if she got up and left? What if she laughed? What if she said, 'I like you, but not like that'?

Eventually, her answer came. 'So do I.' She leaned forward and kissed him lightly on the forehead.

Then, after another pause:

'I would be the happiest man in the world if you would marry me.'

She tensed.

'I haven't given any thought to marriage. Not yet! There's so much I want to do before then.'

'I don't mean now,' he said. 'I can wait. However long it takes.'

The conversation petered out. He did not want to push it.

They sat in silence and listened to Leif's snoring. Then they went inside. He lay down on the floor and she on his bamboo mattress by the window. He tried to sleep, but ended up staring into the darkness. He tossed and turned, then his body became rigid. He listened. She too was moving, unsettled. He wondered if he should say something. Just then, he felt a light gust of air and heard a faint rustling. A soft hand on his shoulder. Almost silently, she crept in under his blanket and lay down beside him on the cold, cement floor.

'You can't sleep either?' she whispered.

'No.'

'I feel scared over there, by the window. Can I lie here with you?'

'Of course,' he stammered.

She moved closer. His desire was reawakened and he grew braver. But she tensed.

'I'll go back to my bed if you can't control yourself,' she whispered gently. 'I didn't come for that. I want you to hold me, that's all,' she added.

So he held her. Who did he think he was? He was ashamed of himself. This was more than enough.

PK and Lotta were lying on the bamboo mat on the cement floor. He looked at her. She seemed so at ease when she slept. He remembered her reaction in the night. She had recoiled at the mention of marriage, but he knew no other way to express his feelings. They could not possibly live together if they were not married, and then the romance would wither. Love could not survive without a solemn vow and an official blessing. At least, that was how he felt. But Lotta wanted to wait, she had told him that much on the veranda. It was difficult for him to understand. If she liked him and her father agreed, why wait? In this, it was obvious they came from different cultures.

But he would keep trying.

'Come with me to Orissa,' he said as they ate breakfast. She gave him a curious look.

'And meet my father. And my sister and brothers.'

'Sure, why not,' she replied.

No counterargument, no questions. But did she really want to come? Had she misunderstood him?

They moved fast, as if they had to act at once, before she could be conquered by doubt. They pushed his things into her backpack and dressed quickly. He pulled on the same dirty trousers and shirt he had worn the day before. It did not feel right when there was a woman in the room, but what else could he do? He did not have any clean clothes.

How bad do I really smell? he wondered.

He turned and looked at Lotta. She was dressed in a newly purchased red sari in a style common to the Varanasi region. That blonde hair and red sari! She was so beautiful.

They took a rickshaw to Connaught Place to buy a gift for his father and some token presents for his siblings. They ate at a Chinese restaurant, threaded in and out of the shops, gazed at each other, laughed. Life was just like the romances he had watched on the big screen, and now they were building towards their climax. But how long before it all came crashing down? As usual, he kept his doubts to himself.

They climbed aboard the Janata Express, and before dusk the long train slithered out of the station and eastwards. A cool breeze wafted through the open window as the sun painted the plains a mango yellow. He watched Lotta's hair flutter in the draught and sometimes whip across her face. He was fascinated by its golden glow in the last light of the day.

Scenes from PK's childhood flickered through his mind. Riding his grandfather's elephant in the jungle at the age of five. His teacher throwing stones at him, shouting that this was his fate. His high-caste friend who was forbidden from playing with him once his parents realized he was untouchable. His thoughts turned to the here and now, as he sat in a train compartment with this beautiful, foreign woman. Characters in the movies were given flashback montages in their dying moments. It was an apt comparison; he was being reincarnated into a better life.

They ordered dinner, which was served at their seats in cardboard boxes. Vegetables, rice and chapati. They sat cross-legged on the green vinyl bunk and ate in silence. It was dark outside, the faint glow of the carriage lighting cast a gloomy blue over them. The train bounced on the rails, the horn bellowed and they rocked back and forth as if on a boat navigating stormy waters.

They climbed up into one of the narrow bunks above and lay close to each other. Lotta tried to read her book about Orissan religious festivals, but soon fell asleep. He lay, gazing at her, breathing in the stillness of her sleep, her closed eyelids, her luminous complexion.

He thought about the conversations they had had over the last few days.

'You've made me believe in God,' she had said to him.

'But I'm poor, I can't take care of you and give you a secure life,' he replied.

'You're not poor to me,' she countered.

'I'm an artist, that means I will never have money.'

'But I want to share my life with you.' It seemed that Lotta had decided to follow her heart after all.

A few hours before dawn, they stepped off the train in Bokaro, the city of steel. This was where PK's oldest brother worked. They huddled close to each other on the dark platform, wrapped in a soiled woollen blanket, and waited in silence for sunrise. Bundles of material scattered around them seemed to accommodate sleeping people. Maybe they were waiting for the train, or, like PK and Lotta, for relatives who would come to pick them up after dawn. They heard barking dogs roving the streets in packs on the other side of the station, and now and then the solitary trumpet of a bus horn.

As the sun rose above the horizon, Lotta went into the station, changed into a new, clean sari and covered her hair with a headscarf. From a distance it was impossible to tell that she was a foreigner. PK was sure that his brother would like her traditional style.

Suddenly, Pramod appeared. PK had not seen him in years. He was now a few kilos heavier, dressed in a Western suit, white shirt and tie. He looked important. He approached with a cautious smile. PK and Lotta knelt before him and greeted him with lowered heads and fingertips to the feet.

Pramod was a division manager on the Indian Railways and was very proud of his position. He was not unique, but it was still uncommon for an untouchable village boy to do so well. Most managers were still Brahmins or from other high castes, despite Indira Gandhi's insistence that state companies had to start obeying the anti-discrimination laws. Pramod's promotion was indirectly Indira's doing.

He showed them his office with its attached kitchen and servants, housed in a railway carriage. On the walls hung portraits of Indira Gandhi and the guru Sai Baba, his benefactor, guardian angel and prophet.

No one believed that PK's brother was the son of a dark-skinned tribal woman and an untouchable man. He was light-skinned and had, rather mysteriously, grown paler with the passing years. The young Pramod had often spoken of his desire to be as white-skinned as a wealthy and powerful European. And now it seemed that his wish had come true. PK knew that black hair turned grey then white with age, but he had never heard of skin getting paler too. But so it was. Pramod looked more and more like the Westerners he so admired, and many in the Soviet-sponsored city of steel treated him courteously, having mistaken him for a Russian guest worker.

PK was worried what his brother would think of Lotta. He did not want to break with local tradition, which decreed that the eldest brother must first approve a marriage, and then the father. He was not sure if it was entirely necessary to follow the custom, but neither did he want to provoke his family unnecessarily. He could not risk being ostracized by them too.

'My oldest and wisest brother,' PK began that first evening, 'may I marry Charlotta?'

Pramod did not answer.

'Charlotta is really the same as Charulata,' PK clarified in Oriya, then turned to Lotta and whispered in English: 'He will probably be more sympathetic when he hears that you have such a nice name. Charulata means vine in Oriya.'

His brother was silent, and then announced that he

needed to think. He would meditate for an hour, during which he would consult with Sai Baba and God.

PK's brother sat down in the lotus position on the cement floor of the living room, surrounded by photographs of snowy mountain peaks and fair-skinned babies. He closed his eyes and his expression turned grave. PK studied his brother nervously, but he could do nothing but wait.

After an hour, a smile broke out across his brother's face. PK knew that it would all be fine.

They took the Madras Express to Tata, switching to the Utkal Express bound for Cuttack and then a long distance coach up the river and into the forest. The vegetation thickened, the sky cleared and the air became easier to breathe. He was back in the village of his childhood. So much had happened since he had last visited.

At once it was clear that his father had no objections to the match.

'You should marry whoever makes you happy,' he said. 'And she fits with your horoscope,' he added.

His father began singing hymns in Sanskrit as if he were a Brahmin. The village priests would surely have been most disturbed by such a display, but Shridhar did not care.

'Why should the Brahmins have the sole right to perform sacred ceremonies?' he used to counter when his colleagues thought he was in danger of provoking the high castes.

PK and Lotta watched. Behind him on the wall hung a portrait of PK's mother. PK felt his Ma's gaze, as though she had returned from the dead, curious to see what he had made of his life.

Then his father brought together their hands, nodded and spoke.

'Pradyumna Kumar,' he said, looking at his son, 'make sure you never give her reason to cry.'

'I promise, as long as she's with me,' he replied.

'If tears run down her cheeks, never let them reach the ground,' his father continued. 'You should always be on hand to comfort your wife.'

Then he presented Lotta with a new sari. It was done. They were husband and wife. They would have to register the marriage formally at the local court, but they could do that later. For now, it did not matter.

With backpacks on their heads, they weaved through the mass of villagers who had come out to see PK and his white-skinned wife dressed in Indian clothes. They had never seen anything like it. They stared unabashedly, but no one dared approach her and say hello. PK's success in Delhi commanded their respect and admiration. He was no longer a pariah.

Rumour spread quickly that the boy from the village who had drawn a cosmonaut, a prime minister and a president had returned. In Bhubaneswar, the secretary-general of the art school invited them to lunch. He praised PK and pulled out their chairs so they might sit down. It was a display completely alien to PK. After lunch, the secretary-general instructed his chauffeur to drive them wherever they wanted to go in town and sent a messenger boy to buy their train tickets. Lotta was presented with a silver hair clasp as if she were a queen. King Pradyumna Kumar and Queen Lotta. It was as if the whole world had transformed into their servants.

They took the bus to Puri and strolled along the wide sandy beach past other lovers, and then on to the Sun Temple in Konark with its carvings of erotic scenes from the Kama Sutra.

Before they reached the Black Pagoda, as the old-time sailors called the temple, PK told Lotta to stop. He cupped his hands and placed them over her eyes.

'Now, for something beautiful.'

He took his hands away.

'Look, up there!'

The temple with the stone wheel. The very same stone wheel in the picture she used to have pinned to her wall in London. She had stared at that picture and longed for India. And now, here she was, standing before the real thing. She started to cry.

They had only met a few weeks before, but here, in front of the temple designed as a chariot for the sun god Surya, their lips touched for the first time.

PK's ecstasy was once again blunted by doubt. It was all so surreal, so detached from reality.

How is it possible for an untouchable jungle boy like me to walk beside the woman I love?

The doubt swelled, occupying everything. He stumbled over the simplest phrases. He fumbled while performing the most basic manoeuvres, such as a caress of Lotta's cheek or avoiding piles of rubbish in the street.

On the bus back to Bhubaneswar he imagined throwing his old life away, the career in New Delhi, for a possible future with Lotta in Europe. He toyed with the idea and it scared him, precisely because it felt so perfectly feasible. Why had he left behind the beauty of his home in Orissa and gone to the capital? This was where his family was, and everything that felt familiar. The jungle was so bounteous, so rich, dense, mysterious and exciting. Mango trees and coconut palms shrouded in morning mist belonged to a landscape that made him question the ingrained notion that it was worth sacrificing everything for the new and the capricious.

As soon as they arrived back at his rented room in New Delhi a week later, his neighbour Didi came to tell him that a well-dressed woman and her daughter had been to visit several times in his absence. Puni and her mother, it transpired. Where was PK? they kept asking. In the end, Didi turned the question on them; why were they looking for him?

Puni's mother told Didi the story:

There was nothing wrong with Puni's fiancé, the engineering student. He was a nice boy. But the boy's father had asked for fifty thousand rupees in dowry. It was an unthinkably large sum, a dowry fit for a film star. Puni's father had been desperate for his daughter to wed the boy from the high-caste family, but eventually he too had to accept that they could not afford it. So Puni's mother had come to see if PK might take her daughter after all.

What an idiotic family! Why would he want anything to do with them, after her father had so humiliated him?

I'm a forgiving person, but there are limits, he thought.

To Didi and his friends, he said that he was already married to the woman from Sweden. This was not strictly true of course. His father had performed the ceremony so that they were united in the eyes of the gods, but they were not technically wed according to the law. But then again, who was going to check something like that?

They spent their nights lying beside each other on the concrete floor of PK's rented room, looking up at the cracked cement ceiling, while Lotta related stories about Swedish history and her ancestors.

'The King of Sweden at that time was called Adolf Frederick and the Queen Louisa Ulrika, and just like India, Sweden had four castes. The King's power had been limited and the country was ruled instead by four parliaments, one for each caste group,' Lotta explained. 'We called them the nobles, the clergy, the burghers and the peasants. Two parties contended for power, and they had the strangest names, the Hats and the Caps!'

'How strange. Imagine that happening in India!' whispered PK. 'People would laugh themselves to death.'

'Let me finish,' Lotta said.

'The King and Queen were furious that the nobles who controlled the Hat Party were attempting to seize power and limit that of the royal family. They even insisted upon raising the heir to the throne, Prince Gustav. This way, the Prince would grow up to be a fair and just king.

'The Queen refused. How could humans alter the will of God? It was madness. She called her advisers and told them about her plan to stop the Hats. They would enact a military coup and reinstate the King, as God ordained.

'One summer evening,' Lotta continued, 'in 1756...'

Just as Robert Clive was struggling to gain dominance over India – what a coincidence, thought PK.

'Have I told you about Robert Clive?' he interrupted. 'I must tell you his story.'

'Later!

'One summer evening, in 1756, chaos broke out in Stockholm. But the details of the Queen's plan had not yet been fully worked out. The agents of the coup did not have the necessary money, and the timing was wrong. But one of the Queen's closest men decided he would start the coup anyway. He collected together his friends and told them to set the plan in motion. Then he ran up the palace staircase to inform the Queen.

'Word of the plan reached the King and Queen's body-guard and a junior officer of only twenty-two by the name of Daniel Schedvin.

'Had he obeyed the order, my family's history would have turned out very differently. Then we wouldn't have owned any forest,' said Lotta.

'You own forest?'

'Not me personally, but my family does.'

She continued. 'The King and Queen's men gathered their troops and marched on the Hat Party headquarters to arrest them. Daniel, however, went to his lord and told him what was going on, and then warned the leader of the noblemen.

'Sweden's warrior caste.'

'We call them Kshatriya in India.'

'The nobility mobilized their opposition and quickly stopped the Queen's attempted coup. The King and Queen were criticized in a sermon given by the high priest. Several others involved were executed. And my ancestor, Daniel, was rewarded with a large sum of money, which he used to buy forest and land. The nobility also forced the King to knight him. To be knighted, that means to change caste and advance upwards,' Lotta explained to an increasingly puzzled PK.

'Daniel became the owner of a large section of the Swedish forest and his family bore a coat of arms decorated in blue and gold, with two crossed swords, a green wreath with ribbons, and a motto in silver: *Ob cives servatus*.'

'What does that mean?'

'It's Latin, but I've forgotten what it means, unfortunately,' she replied.

The family shield was hung in the Stockholm headquarters of his new caste, and in a church in the area where he bought the land.

'That's why my family still owns forest,' said Lotta.

'So you're from a high and noble caste?'

'Yes, that's why my last name is von Schedvin. But I'm not proud of it. It doesn't make me better than anyone else.'

'Lotta, you belong to a high caste while I get less respect than the dirt on the soles of your feet.'

He remembered how Puni's father had shouted at him to leave their house and thought of all the doomed Indian love affairs that ended in honour killings because of similar mismatches.

How was their love affair going to end? he thought as he kissed her on the forehead.

'Yes, but those are just outdated prejudices,' Lotta said. 'That stuff doesn't mean anything to me.'

'You own forest. It's my destiny. If all that stuff hadn't happened all those years ago, the prophecy wouldn't have come true.'

'Yes, you're right.'

'Lotta, you know, everything happens for a reason.'

Lotta took the train to Amritsar, where her friends were waiting with the VW bus. They would go back the way they had come, over the Hindu Kush mountain range, through Iran's deserts and the peaks high above the Black Sea. She recalled the trip they had made only a few months earlier. She remembered how, in the Alps, a guardian angel had prevented the bus from becoming a burning pile of metal at the bottom of a ravine. In Turkey, they wormed their way along endless mountain roads, and the world had never been more beautiful. They almost turned the van to scrap once more in the traffic chaos of Tehran. Hours passed on the roads of Afghanistan without seeing a single person, only empty diners with dusty Coca-Cola signs and no drinks to sell.

Three weeks after their departure from Sweden, they had passed over the border between Pakistan and India. After a detour to the Taj Mahal, they arrived in Delhi late at night, where they collided with a wall and demolished the bumper. It was pitch black and the streets were emptier than usual because of the state of emergency, but they did not know this. They had not phoned home once, but now they contacted the Swedish Embassy and asked the receptionist to call their parents and tell them that they had arrived, having crashed only once, one hundred metres from their final destination. The embassy in New Delhi called through to Borås, but neglected to mention that they had not been injured in the accident.

The trip home to Europe did not worry her, she was now experienced and cleansed. She could have found her way back without a map. The trip went quickly and with no major mishaps, apart from an incident when the van skidded on a patch of ice on a mountain road beyond Trabzon.

They spun full circle and slid to a halt right at the edge of the precipice. But their guardian angel had not abandoned them, and they stepped out of the vehicle, unharmed but in shock.

Everything happens for a reason. And Lotta's destiny was to arrive safely back in Sweden.

It was spring 1976, and at home in Borås, she told her parents that she was in love. PK was the man she wanted to marry, and she would return to India that autumn.

But this time, her mother stopped her.

'PK hasn't finished art school and you haven't got yourself a proper education yet,' came her sober reply. 'Stay here and study. Keep in touch, write letters, get to know each other from a distance.'

It was not what Lotta wanted to hear, but as the memories of India began to fade, as the smells left her clothes, she began to think that her mother might be right. A conflict raged inside her. If she returned now she would surely remain in India, and never come back. But wherever she ended up, she needed a foundation on which to build her life and career.

PK promised he would come to Sweden as soon as he could. But weeks, then months, passed. Their agreed date for a reunion, August, came and went, and PK never appeared. A letter arrived in September from New Delhi. He would come, but he still did not know when exactly, as he was not sure how to get there.

Lotta was reconsidering if she would go back to India after all. She had started work in a kindergarten. The pay was low and she could not save for a ticket. She certainly did not want to borrow money from her parents.

Later, Lotta realized how scared her mother had been that she would not make a career. Women should no longer be only mothers and housewives, her mother said. She had missed out on the opportunity to educate herself, but she would not see her daughters make the same mistake.

New dreams began to take shape. Lotta had learned to play the piano as a child. She applied for a job as a substitute teacher at the municipal music school, as well as for a place at the University College of Music Education in Stockholm.

She got both.

India would have to wait.

PK returned to his previous routine, attending lessons at the art school, painting in the school's studio and drawing portraits by the fountain. But Indian society had changed. New Delhi was paralysed by the new and harsh laws of the emergency: press censorship, slum sanitation, sterilization campaigns, as well as bans on demonstrations and political gatherings.

Bulldozers tore through slums along the city's boulevards and police dispersed crowds. The usually obedient and politically tolerant capital was now boiling over in open rebellion and police repression.

And yet, PK never felt that Indira Gandhi was going too far. If we want to get rid of the corruption and the injustice, then India needed to take a hard line, he concluded. You cannot ask the Brahmins nicely to stop discriminating against untouchables and for employers to start giving them jobs. You cannot expect people to give up their privilege voluntarily, inherited or otherwise, in some false hope that they will act without a stick to encourage them. Politics was the antidote to self-interest, he had learned that from bitter experience.

It had now been over a year since Mr Haksar, Indira's principal secretary, had promised to organize a place for PK to live. Then, in the spring of 1976, Haksar got in touch again.

'It's all done,' he said. 'You're free to move in.'

'Where?'

'South Avenue.'

South Avenue! The road where India's Members of Parliament lived. The exclusive preserve of the country's elite.

'I'm going to live there?'

'Yes,' said Haksar. 'One of the apartments at No. 78 is yours.'

PK packed his belongings, barely filling one bag. He kept his easel and canvases at the fountain and walked all the way to his new home in South Avenue.

The apartment consisted of a large lavishly furnished living room, a separate bedroom, a balcony overlooking the garden, a kitchen, a dining room and two bathrooms. When hunger struck, all he had to do was pick up the phone and food would be delivered straight to his door. When his clothes were dirty, he left them for the Dhobi wallah who came every day to collect them.

One year ago, he had been sleeping under bridges and warming himself by bonfires of rubbish. Now he lived in a bungalow on the same street as the Prime Minister and was never short of money. He must have exhausted his reserve of bad karma; all the fighting and the struggle had filled his well full of better luck to draw on.

For PK, life during the emergency was one of success and increased self-worth. Indira Gandhi was a mother figure for the untouchables, for all of India's oppressed. And sometimes, a mother could be harsh and reprimanding.

She was their benefactor. What would India's untouchables have been without her? Where would he have been without her benevolence? Most certainly, in the gutter.

But PK was still hurting from missing Lotta, and he told anyone who would listen about his loss. The intensity of his feelings so moved people that Lotta received a steady stream of letters from PK, as well as messages from backpackers he met at the Indian Coffee House.

It was as if everyone making the round trip to Asia knew about their story.

Kate from Edinburgh wrote:

I just got back from India. I met your friend
PK while I was out there. He's a nice, honest
guy and he misses you a lot. He was always
talking about you, saying he hopes you
haven't forgotten him. Not that I want to get
involved, of course, but maybe you should
write to him and let him know how you are.

And then a letter from Maria from Bohus-Björkö:

I just got back from Pakistan on Sunday the
6th... I was also in Delhi in January. A friend
from Lahore and I took a short trip to India.
Another friend told us to look PK up and we
did. We met several times and had a great
time. PK gave us a book to give to you... PK
is well, but he misses you a lot.

Beatrice from Pontoise, who thought he was called Pieket,
said:

I arrived home three days ago from Delhi. My
husband and I met Pieket there and he helped
us a lot. Pieket told me about you and we
saw the beautiful photo of you two together.
Pieket asked me to write a letter to you as
soon as I got home to Paris, and it makes me
happy even if my English is poor. I hope you
will understand anyway what I write. Pieket
have not heard from you in two months, and
he is worried about it. He hopes that nothing
happened to you and we hope it too.

PK had everything he had ever dreamed of living somewhere as lavish as the bungalow at 78 South Avenue, and

yet he was miserable. The reason, of course, was obvious. He lay on the bed, looking out at the garden, and thought of how they had walked in the Mughal Garden behind the Presidential Palace and remembered the moment when, among the roses, tulips and temple flowers, he had placed a ring on her finger.

Despite his relative comfort, PK began to become more politically active. He wanted to change the lives of the untouchables with his art. His paintings would force the complacent middle classes to really see and understand their suffering. Outside the Congress Party Head Office, Haksar introduced him to a tall man who shook PK's hand so vigorously he nearly yelped.

The man shared PK's vision, and asked if he wanted to start a magazine for 'the oppressed'.

'Yes,' PK said.

'My name is Bhim Singh. You're the famous fountain painter?' he said.

'Yes,' PK replied again, more gruffly this time. He did not enjoy being treated like a celebrity. 'And what about you, Mr Singh?'

'I have travelled through 120 countries by motorcycle. I have been to Europe, America and Russia and also crossed the Sahara Desert.'

'Most impressive, Mr Singh! But why?'

'For world peace. I'm going to write a book about my experiences.'

'And now?'

'Now I'm going to start a newspaper.'

Singh seemed to be a strong-willed, dedicated man not content to stay in his comfort zone. Nor was he motivated by the pursuit of wealth. PK liked him instantly, and he liked PK.

'Would you be willing to design the newspaper's logo?' Bhim asked.

'Of course.'

'And to illustrate some articles?'

'Gladly.'

Bhim explained that he had already come up with a name: *Voice of Millions*. PK was appointed deputy editor there and then, and Bhim would be editor-in-chief. The two of them made up the entire editorial staff. Bhim would write, PK would illustrate.

They were given a corner of the Congress Party's veranda. Their office comprised a worn typewriter, a broken table and two rickety chairs.

The *Voice of Millions*'s two-man editorial team started work that very week. Every day, they sat on the veranda and composed articles describing the dark side of Indian society, the hunger and the oppression.

'We are the voice of the masses,' Bhim used to declare as fatigue set in and their pace slowed.

PK designed a logo in which the letters of *Voice of Millions* were filled with lots of small, emaciated faces screaming for food. The newspaper of the hungry. A cry against poverty and the caste system. But Bhim did not stop there; he was fighting for another cause as well: the independence of Kashmir. On this topic PK felt less informed, so he left that particular struggle to his friend.

Their first edition was ready. PK took a bundle and went to the streets around Connaught Place. Pride swelled his chest as he carried their newspaper, a newspaper he had helped to create.

He walked a few times around the roundabout, into the side streets, through the park and between the tables of the Indian Coffee House. He walked up to the station, into Paharganj market and then back to the roundabout.

'Get your *Voice of Millions*, the newspaper of the oppressed!' He must have cried this hundreds of times.

'The publication that will change India!' he began to add when no one took any notice.

After two days, he had only managed to sell a handful of copies. He dumped the rest on the pavement, saying: 'Take a copy, it's free! Take it! *Voice of Millions!*'

He returned to Bhim, who was sitting on the veranda, and handed him his resignation.

'India isn't ready for change,' PK said bluntly.

Bhim was not happy with PK's decision, but he decided to continue, at least until the day Kashmir had its freedom.

'Good luck with Kashmir, and the eradication of hunger,' PK said and returned to his easel by the fountain.

There, at least, people took notice and appreciated him.

When anyone Swedish came to the fountain, PK stopped what he was doing and talked to them. If he heard a Swedish voice at the Indian Coffee House, he introduced himself, offering them tea just to have an excuse to sit down and talk about Sweden. He changed his sign at the fountain. Now it said, *Ten Minutes, Ten Rupees. Free for Swedes.*

He wanted as much contact as possible with Lotta's fellow countrymen. Their voices and stories reminded him of her. It was his way of keeping the memories, the feelings, alive, of refusing to let her fade away.

That was how he got to know Lars.

Lars showed PK his Swedish passport and PK drew his portrait for free. He was a journalist and, just like all the others, had travelled overland from Europe to India. He had not driven, but hitchhiked. He thought PK could do the same.

Lars unfurled a map of Asia and together they sat for hours in the café, examining it. He traced his pen along the roads, which were coloured red, and read out the names of the cities. Kabul, Kandahar, Herat, Mashhad, Tehran, Tabriz, Ankara, Istanbul.

'You can make the trip in two weeks, easily. Then you only have Europe left, which you can hitchhike in a week, tops.'

Yes, perhaps I could hitchhike to Sweden, PK thought.

If Lars could, then he could. Three weeks sounded manageable. Sweden had felt like another planet, unreachable for a poor Indian like him. A plane ticket cost a fortune, and he did not dare write to Lotta to ask for money. He did not own a car. But three weeks! It had never occurred to him.

Lars, in turn, was entranced by PK's story of the prophecy and Lotta. He wanted more.

'That's as much as I remember,' said PK.

'There must be more. Try!' Lars said.

'There isn't.'

'It's like a fairytale,' Lars breathed.

One day, Lars told him that a Swedish director was in town, screening a film at the local film festival.

'He could make a movie about your story,' Lars said. 'Sjöman. His name is Vilgot Sjöman.'

'And he's famous?'

'Yes, in Sweden. And in America.'

'As famous as Raj Kapoor?'

'No, more like Satyajit Ray. A serious director. No singing and dancing.'

'What movies has he made?'

'Movies with a political message. And naked people. It was quite controversial.'

Lars wrote down the name of the hotel where the director was staying and told PK to go and introduce himself. But PK was sceptical. Movies with naked people! If the director's reputation was considered questionable in Sweden, imagine what Indians would think! Even kissing was considered too risqué for India. He thought mainly about his family back in Orissa. They would face the consequences if it got out that he had worked with a director who made films about naked people. No, Lars' proposal was not in the slightest bit tempting.

Nevertheless, Lars managed to get him into the film festival, which was being held in the Congress Centre. There, in the crowded vestibule, Lars caught sight of Sjöman. He rushed forward and tapped the director on the shoulder. Then he introduced PK.

The Swede had a nice manner, PK thought. He asked PK what he thought of the state of emergency and Indira

Gandhi and listened carefully to his answers. But PK did not tell him anything personal. He was adamant; no sex tape director was going to make a film about his life. He was not that liberal.

He said goodbye as politely as he could and slipped back into the crowd with a disappointed Lars in tow.

PK was convinced that Lotta would come back. They had agreed upon it. They would be reunited after six months, in August, she said. Either she would come to India, or he would go to Sweden.

He graduated from the College of Art, Delhi, in June 1976 and began to plan for Lotta's return. She can stay with me on South Avenue, he thought. No wife could be dissatisfied with an address like that. No tears would fall on his polished floor.

But he had to find work. He could not sit at the fountain and draw people for the rest of his life.

India Post was looking for illustrators and the art school helped him get an interview. They liked his samples and offered him a six-month in-house training contract in Pune, a city that described itself as cosmopolitan and 'every career-hungry Indian's dream'.

He had a place to live, and a steady job. Or almost. Lotta would be proud of him. India Post also had an agreement with the British Post Office, and the man who interviewed him suggested that there would be a possibility that, if he turned out to be talented and hardworking, eventually, maybe, possibly, he might have the chance to move to London. The very idea of it made him jittery. Imagine living in the colonial capital, together with Lotta!

But August came and went, and Lotta did not arrive. He had neither the time nor the money to make the trip to Europe. His savings were meagre and he was still waiting to start his training.

He waited the whole of autumn to hear from India Post, but nothing came. The disappointment was crushing. But it only made him more determined to be reunited with Lotta.

Their love would have its chance to bloom in person, and not only in finely worded letters. Otherwise, he risked losing her forever.

He organized a new passport and an International Youth Hostel card. Every day, as he made his way to the fountain, he gazed up at the giant billboard for British Airways that had been set up on Connaught Place. It promised another life, on the other side of the planet.

Weeks went by and he grew increasingly unstable from the intensity of his emotions and his longing for Lotta. He found it hard to concentrate, his drawings suffered and he withdrew socially.

One day, he decided to enter one of the main Delhi travel agencies he passed regularly. The girl behind the counter did not look pleased to see him standing before her, dressed in his washed-out T-shirt and jeans. How much for a ticket to Sweden? he asked. Why did he want to know? She had already decided he would never be able to afford it.

'Just tell me what the ticket costs!'

'Almost forty thousand rupees. Do you have that kind of money?'

No, he did not. He had been saving all summer, and yet his bank book showed the grand total of four thousand rupees. What good would all his hard work do? It would take him years.

Perhaps the prophecy had been wrong all along.

PK knew he could either sit around sinking further into despair, or he could make a move. Flying was out of the question: he couldn't afford it. Four wheels? He didn't own a car. Then he remembered Bhim Singh and his journey across 120 countries by motorcycle. Two wheels and a motor? That might be the answer, but it was too expensive. There was another way, though, on two wheels, powered by grit, tenacity and... love.

The Long Journey

New Delhi – Panipat – Kurukshetra – Ludhiana – Amritsar

PK arrives in Kurukshetra in the late afternoon of the first day of his journey. He has been riding since dawn, and decides he has chewed through enough gravel for one day. He dismounts his lady's Raleigh, bought for sixty rupees. Half the price of the men's model. Sixty rupees was a reasonable price for someone like him, who normally struggled to pay for train tickets.

He is on his way to fulfill his astrological destiny. All he has with him is a sleeping bag, a blue windbreaker, an extra pair of trousers given to him by a Belgian postman whom he met in New Delhi, and a blue shirt Lotta had sewn and sent to him. She embroidered his initials on it in the shape of an easel.

He draws his fingers through his dusty hair, rough like bristles on a broom, and squats in the long afternoon shadows of the acacia trees on the outskirts of a small village. He looks out over the fields. The sun sets in the west, so he knows to make his way towards it. Or rather, north-west. But just how many miles he has ahead of him, he has no idea. He has no grasp of the distance, no knowledge of geography. He would struggle to point on a map to all the countries and cities he had heard named in the Indian

Coffee House these past few years.

Stories of the world's creation, the sky and the gods, these he knows better. Tales of the origins of life and its future destiny, even events from the dawn of human history. He recalls the tales of the *Mahabharata*, the book all Indian children are made to read at school, and the great battle between two families that took place here thousands of years ago, right where his bicycle is now resting against a tree, on the outskirts of Kurukshetra. It was a fierce and bitter feud over who would control the kingdom. His teacher at primary school used to read it aloud to them. He enjoys these stories, they are a part of him. In that sense, he is as Indian as it is possible to be.

He looks out over the fields where spears were thrown, swords wielded, blood spilled, and the gods summoned for counsel when doubts crept in. The *Mahabharata* is a book about just war. He recalls a scene in which Prince Arjuna, one of the fighters, pauses and asks the god Krishna for advice. Krishna's response is so long and thorough, it is considered an independent poem. Go back to the field, Arjuna, because you are a warrior, and warriors fight.

It is advice that has been the cause of so much misery. If only they had asked the Buddha or the Jain prophet Mahavira, the world might be a different place.

In Hindi, the road he is travelling is called the Uttarapatha, meaning the northern route. In Urdu, it is known as Shah Rah-e-Azam. The Grand Trunk Road. The backbone of successive empires, a thoroughfare for kings as well as peasants and beggars, Greeks, Persians, Turks and Central Asians. For thousands of years people have taken this route between Afghanistan in the west and the Ganges and Brahmaputra rivers in the east.

Yes, its reputation is both impressive and ominous, but the road itself is not so very grand. Just as narrow and bumpy as every other thoroughfare in India. For two trucks to meet, the same courage and daredevil attitude are required, the same skirting of the asphalt. And along it, the same bellowing monsters of buckled metal slip out beyond the confines of the paved road, throwing up great tempests of sand and gravel that settle in a crackling film over all the other vehicles, pedestrians, grain threshers and ox carts. And bicycles.

Kurukshetra is one of many dreary villages along the way, home to roadside diners hidden behind rows of parked trucks so overfilled with cargo that they look like they might be toppled by the merest prod of a finger. Rickety wooden beds line up beside the trucks, mattresses consisting of nothing but braided rope. Here drivers sit and eat their dinner from metal lunch boxes.

He searches for something that could have borne witness to these ancient stories, but there is nothing old or remarkable about these fields. It's the same monotony of paddies and rows of wheat that have lined the road all the way from New Delhi.

India has been independent for thirty years, and the Prime Minister is trying to remake the country according to her version of Indian socialism. No longer should the people be fooled by superstition and myth. But as far as PK can tell, the legends have not left their mark, at least, not to the naked eye.

He has eighty US dollars sewn into his waistband and a few hundred rupees in his pocket. He must economize. This money has to last him all the way to Kabul, preferably longer. Who knows, maybe with a little luck he can make it all the way to Europe on just this measly sum.

Surely there are people along the way who can help him?

His address book is full of the names of travellers, vagabonds and hippies. Friends. They have described the special community of people bound together and strung out along the hippy trail. We help each other, they said. We share whatever we have. The thought of this big family keeps his nerves in check, even if there is a constant hum in his stomach. The road ahead will be difficult. But he wants it to be difficult, a struggle before a triumph. He wants the tension to drum a beat inside him. It will all work out.

He understands that he must be patient. Save your strength, he tells himself. Sure, he would like to be in Sweden tomorrow. But in the larger scheme of things, he will reach his destination soon. Assuming he makes it that far.

Looking out over the fields, he thinks of his father. Become an engineer, he said. Help build India in Nehru's vision... A memory bubbles up: Nehru and his daughter Indira arriving by helicopter and landing on a beach on the outskirts of Athmallik, there to inaugurate the construction of a new hydroelectric dam on the Mahanadi River. A dot in the sky that grew and grew until it landed next to the buffaloes and cows with their crooked, bony backs. He remembers the bafflement, that something moments before so small could suddenly become so large. 1964, it must have been.

Thousands of people gathered by the banks of the river to catch a glimpse of the Prime Minister. PK remembers Nehru placed his hand on his heart and looked to be in pain. A few weeks later, the Prime Minister died. Perhaps it was no great surprise, the villagers said; the local goddess Binkej Devi must have cursed him. Damming the river was a serious violation of the sacred will of nature, and Nehru had received his punishment.

But PK did not subscribe to such nonsense. He was fourteen at the time and no longer believed everything his elders told him. People died because they got ill. They had been taught that in school.

But just because the world is not governed by gods and demons does not mean there is no cosmic plan. The power of the stars to rule our lives should not be underestimated.

Nehru also had a plan, but a national, not a cosmic one. India was to pursue material wealth and technological progress. Poverty could be eradicated and superstitions and gods were to be replaced by rational thought and science. The nation would put its faith in socialism rather than religion, in Marx and Einstein rather than Vishnu and Shiva. Modernity must take precedence over tradition. If you had to choose, Nehru said, it was better to throw away the old in favour of the new.

And PK's father agreed. This was the best way to be rid of India's injustices. His father did not believe in the old superstitions; he too held firm to reason.

But PK had not become the son his father hoped for. Old injustices have to be replaced by something new and more egalitarian, PK agreed. If anyone hated the traditions espoused by the priests it was him, and yet he never really understood mathematics and science. He preferred to draw people rather than calculate equations. He had learnt it at school, and now, finally, he is escaping all that.

That first night, PK lies in his sleeping bag on the edge of a rice paddy. It is January, and northern Indian winters are cold and damp. He listens as dogs bark and trucks thunder past along the narrow, bumpy road with the grand name. He recognises the smell of stagnant water and watches the breath of the drivers caught in the streetlights. He shivers, zips the sleeping bag around his chin and closes his eyes.

He shuts out the sound of the crickets in the grassy ditch and thinks of Lotta. She knows he is coming. He wrote to tell her about his plan. She replied that if anyone knew the route between India and Europe, it was her.

It was an adventure to drive the VW van all the way to

India and back, and it will be a tough journey for you, she wrote.

Setbacks are often accompanied by crying. As are stories of the humiliation and oppression of others by those in power, or with money and status. PK is known for being governed by his strong emotions. Moments of joy and laughter are often followed by tears. His friends are more balanced and controlled. He envies them. He is unable to regulate his emotions so well.

Anger seizes him sometimes too. He fights them in his daydreams, all the people who have ever humiliated him. But the desire for revenge has softened. More often it is grief that agitates him these days.

He has arrived in Amritsar. But in his diary he writes:

> A week has passed since I was stopped in
> Kurukshetra. Now my Raleigh and the
> Grand Trunk Road have taken me to the holy
> city of the Sikhs with the golden temple. But
> unfortunately it seems that my adventure is
> over. I'm going to go see the golden domes
> and the nectar pond now, then eat dinner in
> the dining room of the temple given out for
> free to the poor before starting my ride back
> to New Delhi. So much for that dream.

Once again, joy has given way to despair. Tears flood his cheeks as a feeling of hopelessness overwhelms him. How can he continue his journey? He is going to have to stop, already. Yesterday, he reached the border with Pakistan. At first, the border guards had refused to let him in. No Indians allowed, they said. Not under any circumstances. They tossed his passport back at him and told him to turn around. But he took out some of the drawings he had made and showed them to the police. He could draw portraits of them, he suggested. Reluctantly, they agreed, and he took out paper and a piece of charcoal. He talked as he drew, telling them about the woman he loved and the country he was going to make his home. Their expressions grew ever more curious, and they began to relax.

It was a great story, and as soon as they saw their grim faces appear on the paper, they smiled. All severity was blown away. Just as he had hoped. It usually worked. To be drawn is to be seen at your best, to be flattered, and it softened even the thickest of skins most of the time.

'Okay, we'll let you ride through our country,' one of the Pakistani officers said.

'Are you sure we can do that?' another countered in Urdu, a language of which PK had passing knowledge.

'Yes, yes, what does it matter? He looks like a kind soul.'

They turned to PK and the man who seemed to be second in command said politely: 'On you go, sir!'

They opened the bar and he rode into Pakistan.

Half an hour later, he swung his bicycle into a leaky wooden shed with charpoys and glossy painted tables. He got down, and feeling pleased with himself, approached a man with a bare head and sullen countenance who sat in the shade of the jute awning, next to a cabinet of bulbous sweets clouded in a swarm of flies.

He ordered a huge plate of chicken biryani, and gulped down his first meal across the border, sitting on the edge of a charpoy.

He burped, washed his hands, and filled his canteen. Then, just as he mounted his bicycle to continue on, a police jeep swung into the yard in front of him.

'Passport, passport!' shouted one of the officers as he jumped out of the rolling vehicle.

PK pulled out his green passport with the King Ashoka lion on the cover, *Bharat Ganarajya* written in golden

Devanagari script and *Republic of India* in English. They flipped through its pages, from back to front and vice versa, before closing it and turning it upside down. They shook their heads.

The police then pointed to the bike and then to the jeep. PK understood what was being said. They threw the bike on the roof, told him to take a seat in the back, and proceeded to drive him to the border crossing.

All he had to do was ride the fifty kilometres back to Amritsar in India.

If the road to the future had already been determined, it was turning out to be peppered with pitfalls, thought PK, as if some higher power had decided that paradise could only be reached after first conquering seven earthly trials.

He sits on the hostel bed and watches the sun go down behind the rooftops, listening to the cries from the minarets drowning out the crows in the banyan trees. Hope has stirred in him again. His luck has returned.

That morning, he caught sight of a familiar face in the crowd at Guru Bazaar. It was Mr Jain! He worked in the Ministry of Information in Delhi. They had first met a few years before, and it turned out he was also a friend of PK's older brother. And here they were, bumping into each other in Amritsar.

As the melancholy sound of the minarets chases the darkness into his hostel dormitory, he feels fortunate to know such an educated, high-ranking man.

But he should have met him the day before yesterday. Then he would have dispelled some of PK's misconceptions. For example, that PK would be able to enter Pakistan, when Indian citizens were blanket forbidden, even when long-haired, pot-smoking hippies from America and England were welcomed with open arms into the Islamic Republic.

He knew he would need a visa for the Shah's Iran. But to Pakistan? India and Pakistan, two countries that were once one, that shared virtually the same culture, food and language, the same customs. Why was there even a border at all? But he should have known. He is ashamed by his ignorance. The conflict between India and Pakistan filled the papers daily: how could he have missed it?

But in Guru Bazaar that morning, Mr Jain had felt sorry for PK and announced that he wanted to buy him a plane ticket so that he could fly to Kabul without having to cycle through Pakistan. Fly high above the border police and all the earthly problems below.

'On me,' he said. It was the least he could do. 'You're not just anyone, after all. I've read about you in the newspaper.'

PK bowed deeply, shook his hand, knelt down and touched the man's feet. His lucky cobra, the snake that had been protecting him since he was born, had come to his aid again.

He meets a German hippy at the hostel and shows him the flight ticket. The German is on his way back to Europe with his wife. They are driving a minibus furnished with beds and a small kitchen.

'Okay, Picasso, we'll take your bike to Kabul on the roof of our van.'

They give him a cloth pouch to hang around his neck. 'To keep your passport safe,' he explains.

Now PK looks almost like all the Germans and other Europeans he has been meeting these last few years. A backpacker, one of the gang out on the hippy trail.

The engines roar. He is pressed into the back of his seat, feels a tickle in his stomach. Later, he would reflect on the moment in his diary:

> I look down at Earth from the aircraft and
> am filled with what I see, the snow-capped
> mountains, the arid steppes, the green fields;
> they are all larger and more true than my
> own life. Everyday problems seem petty from
> this height, the possibilities are endless and
> life is as wide as the sky. Worries are nothing
> but dots on a map.

Through the aeroplane window he looks down on empty cities, pavements with no people, roads with no cars.

'Up in the sky, it is difficult to make out the details down on Earth,' he writes. 'This is the first time I travel with a flying machine. I travel far away never to return. I can still not really believe it, but it looks like the prophecy came true.'

Amritsar – Kabul (almost) – Amritsar (again) – Kabul (finally)

Something is wrong. Just as they were about to land in Kabul, the plane started climbing and now they are circling the airport. Nervous, PK gazes out at the brown carpet scored with a grid of roads below. They go even higher and then start flying straight. The shaking ceases and is replaced by an otherworldly murmur. No one says anything over the speakers. After an hour, they are ready for landing and start their descent again.

As he looks out, he sees that they are back in Amritsar. There has been no explanation, and he is too scared to ask. Maybe the weather was too bad in Kabul? Maybe there was a hole in the runway?

He is back in India. Again.

But this time, he does not feel hopeless. They are put up in a luxury hotel at the airline's expense and given tickets to eat at the gourmet buffet several times a day. The Air India staff make an appearance and promise that flights to Kabul will resume the next day. And he is not disappointed. The next morning his journey restarts, and finally, he lands in Kabul.

The shuttle bus drives along empty boulevards towards the city centre. The roads are edged by trees that have lost their leaves. There is so little traffic in contrast to back home in India. Not that same urban crush. Light grey mountains rest on the horizon, standing against a crisp blue sky.

His mind returns again to Lotta as he watches Kabul slip past the window. This time last year, they were standing together at the railway station in Delhi, about to say good-bye. She was taking the train to Amritsar to meet up with her friends, where they were waiting with the VW van. She was bound for Europe, he was stuck in India. A thick voice came over the tannoy: *Two Nine Zero Four Golden Temple Mail bound for Amritsar is at platform number one.* The stationmaster rang the bell and blew his whistle, the signal at the end of the platform went from red to green and steam from the engine blasted up high above them.

'It sounds like a bomb going off,' Lotta said, and kissed him one last time before climbing onto the train.

'Yes,' PK laughed, not yet shattered by his grief.

She hung in the doorway as the train started to roll. He intertwined his left hand in her right, pressed his cheek against hers, and walked quickly as the creaking carriages gradually accelerated. He was so distracted by the softness of her hand and cheek that he did not see the rapidly approaching fence at the end of the platform. Their grand farewell ended as the metal poles struck against his chest, and he fell over. He screamed in pain, scrambled onto all fours, and watched the train disappear as his tears spotted the cracked cement beneath his hands and knees.

The train was gone. Lotta was gone. His future had been ripped from him and was disappearing into the distance.

He cried all the way from the station to the usually crowded street bazaar at Chandni Chowk, now desolate at this hour, just before midnight. He walked under Tilak Bridge and passed Delhi's old dilapidated fort and zoo, where they had walked only a few days earlier, holding hands. Lotta had been sitting beside him as he painted watercolours of the ruins and caged animals.

A pack of dogs, growing bolder now the sun had set, started rounding on him. They bared their teeth, barked, and drew close. But PK was not scared. Instead, he stopped, planted his feet, took a deep breath and yelled back at them.

'Eat me then, you mangy mutts! Eat me! I don't care!'

The dogs closed in, slowly. But something in their growling made PK imagine they were pondering what he had just said. They fell silent and wagged their tails. He opened the remains of his lunch, wrapped in a crumpled newspaper, and fed some of it to them. He sat among the dogs as they ate. All energy had gone from his body and he was numb, exhausted by the crying and the long walk. He lay down on the ground and the dogs rested their heads against his body.

That night, PK and five of Delhi's fiercest stray dogs huddled together on the pavement outside the city zoo. In his dreams, wild storm winds tore houses from their foundations and violent waves came crashing over him.

Before dawn he was awakened by the shrill screech of shock absorbers and the rattling of chassis as the first morning buses sped past. He sat up and looked around him, dazed. A cold wind had swept away the last of the previous day's heat. He felt chilled. The dogs, his blanket in the night, had disappeared.

He stumbled the last kilometres home to his rented room in Lodi Colony, where he was still living at the time. He stood in the doorway and looked in on the miserable scene inside: a worn bed, a dresser and a calendar depicting Lakshmi, the goddess of happiness and wellbeing, clinging to the mould-flecked wall.

As Lotta journeyed westward, PK waited for the merest sign of life from her. But his letters went unanswered.

Desperate, he sent telegrams to her home address: 'I'm worried by your long silence, please write to me when you get back home. PK.'

But Lotta was still on the road. Finally, a letter arrived from Maku in western Iran. 'My dear friend and companion,' it began. He read it quickly, starved of her words. The letter described the magic journey, the beauty of the snow-capped mountains on the border between Iran and

Turkey, the pale sun, the serenity of Maku, the transparent cold mist and 'the buzz of insects, nature's lullaby'.

She wished he could be with her, the letter concluded.

But then why did she leave?

Lotta's beautiful, poetic letters were unsettling; their mood somehow made him even sadder. Her long, engaged descriptions of places so completely alien carried almost a sinister tone.

He climbs down from the airport bus and starts walking through the throngs of men in ankle-length shirts and women with scarves wrapped around their heads, through the bazaars, and out onto the street with the funny name – Chicken Street, or Khosheh Murgha as the Kabul locals call it. There he finds a cheap-looking hostel.

All the wanderers gather here, with their long hair and their backpacks. They are dirty and bedraggled, as if they have been dragged through all the filthy streets of the world. His hostel is followed by another and another, countless English signs promising cheap accommodation and great service. Then comes a row of cafés and restaurants, menus also in English. He looks out along the street; for every Afghan in traditional dress he can see a white person in tight jeans and a T-shirt.

PK has been recording the trip so far in his diary with the intention of sending extracts to the newspapers in Orissa. He is confident they will be interested.

'Tens of thousands of Western hippies are heading East and West at any given time, whether they have been in India and are on their way home to Europe or vice versa,' PK writes. The cafés of Chicken Street are abuzz with stories of the road to Kandahar, where to stay in Herat, the best coffee shops in Mashhad, the top bargains in the markets of Istanbul and how to cope with the traffic chaos in Tehran. A Frenchman explains the itinerary to PK as they drink tea.

'The hippy trail,' he clarifies, 'isn't one single road, but in fact many that interlock.'

PK shares a room with four Europeans. It feels like they belong together. Everyone helps each other. He has met several of the other guests before in New Delhi.

'Hey, PK!' he hears people call out on the street, from cafés, in bazaars.

He hugs them, drinks cup after cup of tea, tells them what he's been up to and where he's going and listens to their stories in return. He asks about their upset stomachs, while they tell him how brave he is and how they wish him well on his long journey.

Some of the European girls wear shorts. The Afghan men stare so they do not see where they are going, colliding with each other on street corners. A Swedish girl he met several times in India walks towards him in thin balloon pants with bells around her feet. She is a thrilling sight for the local men, as she tinkles past like a tambourine. The men laugh and cast their eyes up to the heavens.

He is reluctant to rip open the seam in his trousers and start on the eighty dollars he has stashed. He is saving them. So he goes to give blood, as it is well paid. And he sits in the teahouses drawing people. It always works. People are curious, approach him, start asking questions, and are delighted when they see the results. It looks just like him! They laugh, point and shake his hand. They want to be drawn too, when he is done. And they pay handsomely.

The editor from *The Kabul Times* is impressed. He wants to see the other drawings leaning against the cement wall under the coffee table. PK shows him Afghan tribal women with their heavy silver jewellery and nose rings, as well as bearded Bedouin riding camels. The editor says he wants to interview him.

'Of course,' PK replies. He is used to journalists and knows the importance of publicity for a struggling artist.

The interview appears a few days later. The picture shows PK holding up one of his paintings of an emaciated black woman breastfeeding her equally starved child next to a white statue of the Virgin Mary and plump baby Jesus. *Faces fascinate me, says Indian portraitist*. The text is both courteous and admiring in tone:

> Pradyumna Kumar Mahanandia was the unusual caller at *The Kabul Times* offices last week. On his way to a round the world tour, the young portraitist from India came to Kabul recently on a fortnight visit.
>
> 'Faces fascinate me more than anything else. They attract me, vex me, provoke me,' says the soft-spoken, unassuming Mahanandia. His strongest desire is to paint human tragedy bringing out the inequality of one being and another. 'No matter rich or poor, all are starving for something or other,' he says.
>
> He earns a living from making sketches. 'I want to specialize in portraits and miniatures. Sketching is just a side business to keep myself going,' he added.
>
> 'To make his living is as important for the artist as to pursue his art,' says Mahanandia and is very emphatic about it...

PK laughs. Did he really say that? Yes, probably. He continues reading:

It is the first time that the young Indian artist has visited Kabul and he is overwhelmed with the natural beauty of the place. He has met a number of artists in Kabul and seems quite impressed by their talents and works.

Mahanandia began school as a science student but soon proved a flop and instead took up studies in art, which he had been practising since the age of three...

Mahanandia observes: 'Few people are willing to invest money in a landscape or in a modern painting, but no one minds spending a few pennies on a self-portrait. Everyone has an egotistic streak in him that makes him want to see himself on paper. It is a perfect combination for a needy man.'

The article attracts attention. People on the street turn around and point; some come up and say hello. The journalist returns to PK's hostel and tells him that the editorial board has decided to exhibit some of his drawings in the newspaper canteen.

PK finishes hanging his paintings and steps back, looking pleased with the results. The journalists gather and examine his work. They seem interested, he thinks. The editor buys several of his drawings. The money is good. Very good.

Now, he has enough to last him all the way to Europe.

He has already received his bicycle from the German couple who drove it on their van from Amritsar. It is parked outside the hostel, but the chain is sluggish and squeaky, so he decides to spend some of his freshly earned cash on a new bike from one of the workshops on Chicken

Street. He trades in his Raleigh and pays the difference.

The new bike is red.

PK stays two weeks in Kabul, meeting old friends and gaining new ones. He may be an unusual figure among the backpacker community, with his dark brown complexion, but somehow, he feels included in their gang. Why have they accepted him? Because despite initial differences, he wears the same clothes as them, has grown his hair and speaks good English. But above all, he is an artist: the sketchbook and pencils are his entry ticket into the white world of the hippies. He is a mascot, a bohemian splash of colour in a world of rebellious middle-class Westerners.

He sits on a small stool, a sketchbook on the table and pens in his shirt pocket, and is bought tea, chicken, rice and yogurt. Evening after evening is spent like this, in his favourite restaurant, talking to other travellers and occasionally drawing them, or Afghans passing on the street outside.

They are so free, the backpackers. Anything is possible while in their company, everything is open for discussion and everyone is entitled to their opinion. It is so unlike back home in India, where people are constantly trying to work out where you are from and who your parents are. These vagabonds of Chicken Street are becoming his new family. They are his brothers and sisters, friends through thick and thin, not bound by tradition or prejudice. He learns that they have left home in search of something deeper than the materialism of where they come from.

'Factories operate at capacity, everyone has jobs, we all have enough to eat and we are surrounded by stuff we don't really need,' an American backpacker tells PK as they sit opposite each other, drinking tea.

His name is Chris and he comes from California. The

restlessness he embodies started in the detached houses of the suburbs and grew into a fury over an unjust war in Vietnam. Young people, just like PK's new friends in Kabul, gathered in parks to protest the injustices of the existing world order.

'Love won out there,' explains Chris. 'And then it conquered the city, took over the country, ended the war, and began to spread right across the rest of the world. That's why we're here now,' Chris continues, as they sit surrounded by other Westerners in Indian cotton trousers and brightly coloured T-shirts. 'Look around you. What you see is the embodiment of love. People like you and I can end all the hatred of the world. We are an army of deserters. We put flowers in the barrels of our guns. Yesterday America, Kabul today, tomorrow India and the rest of the world,' he announces confidently.

PK recalls how hatred and mistrust still linger in India, despite Mahatma Gandhi's speeches preaching nonviolence. His home country may need more love pilgrims. Indians who talk about love, such as the Brahmins, are false prophets. They do not know what love is. If the Brahmins really understood the meaning of the word, PK thinks to himself, then they would never treat untouchables like me the way they do. But hippies? They seem to practise what they preach.

He sits on the bed in his hostel and writes letters to Lotta. The minarets call out for evening prayer.

'From my window I can see mountains covered with snow,' he writes. 'But the cold weather doesn't affect me. My heart feels warm because of the love from you, forever. Your love makes me joyful, always.'

Despite his longing to see Lotta, he is reluctant to continue his bicycle trip. He wants to rest first, meet other travellers and get more tips about the best route to take. And he needs a visa for Iran and that takes time, they say. But he has not even made the journey across the city to the Iranian Embassy to fill out the application. He was refused once in New Delhi, and he dreads another no in Kabul. What will he do then? Ride his bike through the Soviet Union? Was that even possible?

A young Australian woman by the name of Sara is also staying at the same hostel. They spend several afternoons together, sitting on the wooden chairs in the lobby, chatting about their travels, India and life in general. The sounds of Kabul's minarets bounce along the narrow alleys between the houses. Twilight descends and the shops on Chicken Street pull down their steel shutters for the night. And they talk for hours, forgetting to go out and eat while restaurants are still open. By the time they realize they are hungry, it is too late. The people of Kabul go to bed early, and now everything is closed. But what does it matter when there is so much to talk about?

'The West is doomed; the future belongs to Asia,' Sara says.

'For me it's the opposite. My future lies in the West,' PK replies.

And yet they have so much in common.

Sara takes him to a nightclub. It is his first time. She wears a yellow dress with a red spiral batik pattern, he wears the blue flared trousers the Belgian gave him in New Delhi and the shirt Lotta embroidered with his initials. Everyone looks at them. A dark guy with wild, tousled hair and a light-skinned girl. To the Afghans, they are an exotic couple. Maybe even sinful. They have never seen anything like it. He recognizes their envious, covetous glances. They dance to 'Yes Sir, I Can Boogie', 'Rivers of Babylon' and 'Dark Lady'. Just as the rich tones of Marvin Gaye come through the speakers, a man in a suit and neatly done-up tie approaches. He looks PK in the eye.

'May I dance with your girl?' he asks.

My girl?

'She's not my girlfriend. We're just friends,' PK replies. The man is polite. Sara looks at PK and nods. So he goes and sits down by himself at a table next to the dancefloor while Sara follows the man into the depths of the pulsating throng.

They dance and PK watches. As the evening draws to an end and the nightclub is about to close, Sara comes to his table. Her dance partner is Iranian and he wants her to go home with him. He works at the Iranian Embassy and owns a nice apartment in Kabul.

Who is PK to object? She is allowed to do what she wants. They are not married, they are not even together. But he is concerned for her, tells her to be careful, to be on her guard.

PK walks alone under the stars, back to Chicken Street.

Sara will be back at the hotel the next morning and they will continue their conversation then.

Sara comes running into the lobby, where PK is reading *The Kabul Times*.

'Come on, hurry up!' she cries. 'The Iranian works in the embassy's visa section. They're going to get you a visa, but you have to come now.'

Sara and PK are sitting in the back of a car with diplomatic plates and tinted windows, feeling important. They are usually nomads, living and travelling by simple, modest means. But now they feel like VIPs on a state visit.

In the car, Sara tells PK that she spent the night putting pressure on the Iranian to get him the visa. Sara is too kind, PK thinks.

They go to the embassy officer's apartment in the outskirts of Kabul. The driver parks the car, asks them to wait and goes in with PK's passport. He returns quickly, smiling, and hands the passport back to PK, who flips through to find the long-awaited visa.

But the stamp in his passport grants him only fifteen days' transit.

I'll have to ride fast, he thinks.

Kabul – Sheykhabad – Ghazni – Daman – Kandahar

He is travelling ever further away, but at the same time, he is on his way home. Fate has spoken. The prophecy was correct.

In his mother's youth, while PK was tucked up inside her womb, she had dreamed of a baby sitting on a cloud, drifting away. He is not sitting on a cloud now exactly, rather the new red bike he bought in Kabul, on his way south towards Kandahar. Grey mountains daubed with patches of snow stand out against the red of the horizon. He is surrounded by a lunar vista, the desert reaching out towards the sunset. The sky is blue, the air crisp and clear, the Russian-built concrete road ashen, straight and smooth. It beats a rhythm every time he cycles over the joints. Thump, thump, thump. Monotonous and unnerving, it makes him dizzy.

He watches his shadow. The further the sun rises in the sky, the shorter it becomes, but it never leaves him. It is his constant companion, day after day.

I am not alone, the shadow is my friend. It never lets me down.

He is spurred on faster as his shadow grows longer. He is not standing still, even though the landscape feels uninterrupted and unchanging. The length of his shadow tells him he is making progress.

He stops to rest. All is strangely silent: he can hear no birds, no insects, no trucks, no rustling of trees. There are no trees here. Afghanistan is desolate, just gravel and stone. A world on mute, where only the wind occasionally speaks to break the silence. The heat wobbles above the tectonic plates of cement. This place is so different, it makes him wonder: have I landed on another planet? He feels lonely but it does not bother him. Rather, it gives him peace. Is this how it feels to leave my homeland?

Suddenly, he spots a small group of Afghans standing by the side of the road. They are talking loudly, sound indignant, outraged even. There, halfway down the ditch, two cars lie crumpled in a heap, with broken windshields and dented hoods. He approaches and the smell of petrol fills his nostrils. Then he sees her. A girl, lying on a woollen blanket in the gravel. She is still conscious, but looks battered. Blood is pouring from her mouth and her forehead is covered in wounds. He bends down and looks at her. He asks her name and where she comes from. But she cannot speak. Her teeth have been knocked out and her lips are cut. He looks at her clothes and realises she too is a backpacker. She is white. A European heading home after an Indian adventure, perhaps. A strong feeling comes over him; he must help her. He must repay the kindness. She is one of his new family, the community of vagabonds, and you cannot leave a sister in need.

They hitch a ride on a truck back to Kabul. The bike, his bag and the white girl's rucksack and cotton bag with the Devanagari print have been thrown into the open cargo. The driver hums an Afghan song PK does not understand.

He is travelling back the way he came, the last two days of cycling will have been in vain, and yet he feels strangely elated. The twilight sun has turned the usually tough, brownish-grey desert peachy warm and silky soft. The truck's rumbling engine is also singing, 'Onward, onward,' even though he is actually travelling backward, backward, and the driver's song seems, in some mysterious way, to be whispering promises to him. He closes his eyes and imagines his own translation to the Pashtun lyrics: 'Be whatever you want, anyone you want. Be your own fate, make your own future.'

Lulled by the monotony of the landscape, he suddenly sees his mother sitting beside him in the truck. She is warm and soft. He feels her presence and hears her steady breathing. Her phantom hand brushes against his right side and he feels tears of happiness, sadness and longing pool in his eyes. If she had still been alive he might never have started this journey. Now there is nothing keeping him in India, only forces pulling him away.

He turns his head towards the feeling. Of course, there is no dark, round, safe mother, but instead a much leaner young girl. Yet her bruises remind him of the lines and dots tattooed on his mother's cheeks, forearms and hands.

The hospital in Kabul confirms that not only has the young woman lost nearly all her teeth, but she is suffering from a serious concussion. She still has trouble talking and the sores make it painful for her to move her mouth. She writes him a note instead. *My name is Linnea*, it says. *Please stay with me!* she adds.

'I will, I promise,' PK responds. 'Where were you going?'
Home she writes.
'Where's that?'
Vienna.
'You'll probably have to wait, you can't go home all bruised like this.'

But Linnea wants to leave as soon as possible. She is back on her feet after two days and is discharged from the hospital. He goes with her to the Austrian Embassy and they organize a plane ticket back to Vienna. She had been driving her own car when the accident occurred, but it was totalled and she is in no condition to drive.

He goes with Linnea to the airport and takes in the details of her face before it is time to part. She smiles her toothless smile and writes one final note: *See you soon!* And then she locks him in a long, warm embrace.

He does not feel particularly noble or good as he rides the bus back to Chicken Street and to the same budget hostel he left only days before. He expects no chorus to sing his praises. The choice to help Linnea was an obvious one. How could he expect help if he refused to give it to others? Emotions can be rational sometimes. Cause and effect. Everything is connected. It was as simple as that.

And he will need help, he knows that. He does not even know if he is supposed to turn left or right or keep going straight ahead once he gets to Kandahar.

Three days later, PK is heading south on the wide cement road between Kabul and Kandahar for the second time. Now he hopes that he has left Chicken Street and the backpacker cafés of Kabul for good, that he is on his own again. He and his red Hero bike. It rides well, but after the first day's cycling he has a headache from pounding over the seams between the cement plates of the road. How is he going to cope all the way to Kandahar? His thoughts hover in daydreams as his exhausted body works on autopilot. Only Lotta's letters, the words she always uses, drum in his chest. My dearest, my dearest, my dearest.

Kandahar

PK meets another Belgian in one of the Kandahar's luxury hotels. PK tells him that he has come from Kabul and is on his way to Borås. On a bike.

'You've cycled all the way from Kabul?' the Belgian asks.

'Do you think that's far?' PK answers with a question.

'Yes, it's five hundred kilometres. That's a long way by bike. And you're going to ride several thousand kilometres further to…? What was it called? Borås? Where's that? In… Switzerland?'

'Yes.'

'Are you sure?'

'Yes, Borås is in Switzerland,' PK says.

The Belgian looks at him questioningly.

'Are you sure?'

'One hundred per cent.'

But the Belgian is not so certain. PK shows him Lotta's letter.

He reads, then takes out a map. 'Here!' he says after a while and points to a spot on the paper. 'This is Borås.'

'Yes. In Switzerland, no?'

'No, Sweden,' says the Belgian and laughs.

'You pronounce it a little differently, but aren't they the same place?'

'They are two different countries,' the Belgian says firmly.

Now it is PK's turn to look sceptical. 'Are you sure?'

The Belgian shows him on the map. He's right. How stupid could he be? She told him she was Swedish. But he had thought Swedes lived in a country called Switzerland. And then he remembers her words:

'No, we don't make watches in my country. My city is famous for weaving fabric.'

He is thoroughly embarrassed, and puts it down to never having examined such a detailed map before. The Belgian's had every road marked and labelled with a number, and it was overlaid with a grid that gave exact latitudes and longitudes. PK had only ever read those crude atlases for sale in the markets of India. They were completely useless for a cyclist wanting to find his way between New Delhi and Borås. He had got this far by asking.

At least he is going in the right direction.

'Aren't I?'

'Yes,' the Belgian confirms.

But PK cannot just blame bad maps.

He had most definitely believed that the inhabitants of Switzerland called themselves Swedes and anything from Switzerland was Swedish. But no, Swedish people came from Sweden. But why come up with two such similar sounding names? It was a recipe for confusion.

Maybe this whole plan was a stupid mistake. How could he not even know where he was going? It was more hopeless than he had first thought.

'How much further is Sweden from Switzerland?' he asks the Belgian.

'About one and a half thousand kilometres more,' he replies.

PK goes to the post office and asks to look through the cardboard box of poste restante. A light blue aerogram is waiting for him. Rejoicing, he opens it.

'My dearest PK...'

He drinks in her words like a thirsty camel drinks water.

> Time is almost 9.30 p.m. I've been horse
> riding continuously for six hours. PK, to be

honest, I'm a bit worried to learn about your plans to go by road all alone from India. We were four adults travelling together, when something happened to us or the car we could always defence each other, but if you go on your own, who will help to defence you when your self-defence isn't enough?

He thinks about her warning. He should be travelling with someone. The route from India to Europe is no game, especially not for the solo traveller. She's right. But he does not have anyone to do the journey with, that is the problem. He has only his sleeping bag and his bike for companionship. But he is sure it will work out. He has his easel, a smile and an ability to make friends even among his worst critics.

And yet, he wants the trip to be tough. It should not come too easy. The road to Lotta must be paved with adversity. Only then will it feel authentic. Aches from the saddle, exhaustion every time he puts his bicycle down in the afternoon, relief to fill his belly with food and lay his body in a hammock, to stretch his legs, dispel negative thoughts and fight to keep the doubt and homesickness at bay.

It is too expensive to fly, but more than that, it would be too easy. That is how the rich travel, but not him. He is a drifter, a vagabond. So far, he has overcome all the obstacles put in his way. Sword in hand, Alexander the Great had made his way along the same route, admittedly in the opposite direction. But PK is travelling with a pencil. His battering ram.

'I understand that you have met many helpful people along the way. You are able to reach people with your paper and pencil. When I think about that, I'm not so worried,' writes Lotta.

PK decides to keep focused on the end goal. Soon, we will be reunited.

Kandahar – Delaram

Afghanistan feels both modern and ancient at the same time. The roads are neat and straight, something he has never seen in India before. Even the Grand Trunk Road is just rubble compared to this, he thinks. But Afghanistan is a strange place. He sees almost only men out on the streets, and the women who do venture out are hidden underneath a thick layer of material.

As is his way, he quickly makes new friends. It comes naturally to him; he does not need to think about it. He jokes with the people he meets. It always breaks the ice; a laugh bridges language and cultural differences. And then he draws them. He works fast, first just a sketch, which he shows them. It never fails. Even policemen and soldiers break out in smiles when they see his drawings.

He is invited home by one of the head doctors at Kandahar hospital. He has seen PK's portraits on the streets of the city and wants him to draw one of his four wives.

'Of course!' PK responds, and cycles there the following day with a stick of charcoal, a bundle of pencils and a pad of paper in a bag dangling from the handlebars.

The doctor's house is palatial. He must be immensely rich, PK thinks as the butler opens the door. He is let in and shown around by the doctor himself, who is at pains to explain that the furniture has been imported from Paris and no luxury is too much for him and his wives.

PK walks into a circular room crowned by an immense semi-circular sofa. This is where the doctor's first, second and third wives are sitting. Their faces are uncovered, a rare sight in Afghanistan. Perhaps they only need to wear burqas when going outside, PK reflects. He greets them in turn, putting his hands together and bowing: 'Namaste.'

The three wives return the greeting with curious looks and mumbled hellos.

Then, a figure enters. A walking tent, but somewhere deep inside the burqa there is, PK assumes, a person. The doctor points to the fabric and he understands: this is his fourth wife, and PK will be drawing her.

PK is left alone in a side room, facing her. He is petrified, unable to bring himself to draw a piece of cloth. But then she starts talking. He is flabbergasted. The voice speaks perfect English with a clear American accent. If he closes his eyes he would have assumed she was an American tourist.

She removes the burqa. He is even more surprised. She is wearing a tight T-shirt, jeans and high-heeled shoes. A thick layer of make-up has been painted on her face and the sweet smell of perfume hangs like a cloud around her. But she cannot be older than fifteen. She is beautiful, very beautiful even, in complete contrast to the dull, heavy fabric of her covering. But her age saddens him. He thinks of her husband, the head doctor. Sixty-four, wrinkled, bald and with a fat belly. The poor girl! What a miserable future!

His sorrow then turns to anger. These outdated traditions, polygamy and arranged marriages, they have to be stopped. Love cannot be planned and controlled. Love must be free. In the future, the people of Afghanistan and India must be able to choose for themselves who they will marry.

He tells himself that he is the happiest Indian in the world. Unlike the girl sitting opposite him, he took his chance and broke with tradition. But then the uncertainty of it all comes back to him. His separation from Lotta, the unbearable longing, the journey. Is he really happy?

At least the doctor's young wife knows her lot. What is he heading towards? Will he ever reach the remote town of Borås and be reunited with Lotta? And will he ever see his father and siblings again?

He is free, he is unburdened. But he is also driven to pedal every day until he almost collapses with exhaustion. In fact, he is also one of the loneliest Indians in the world. The anxiety is physical, a constant tingling sensation just below his lower left rib. The more he thinks about how vulnerable he really is, the more it eats at his sense of freedom and his hopes for future happiness. Maybe Lotta was right. This journey is far too dangerous to undertake alone.

The girl's husband keeps popping his head in, asking when he will be done. He should really start now. But he cannot, his mind is spinning and he feels paralysed. Instead, he asks the beautiful fourth wife:

'Are you happy?'

'Yes, I'm happy,' she answers quickly.

'But your husband, do you really love him?'

'Yes.'

'In your heart?'

'I really love him.'

'But do you think he loves you?'

'Yes.'

'But he has three other wives.'

'He loves me most.'

'How do you know that?'

'I get whatever I want. I just have to point. If I want a new perfume from Paris, he makes a call and then a week later it arrives in the mail.'

'But wouldn't it be better to marry a boy your own age?'

'I don't trust men my age, they say all kinds of pretty things, tell you they love you, but they never keep their promises.'

She sounds brainwashed, he thinks, but he does not say this.

'He only sleeps with me, not the other three,' she says.

PK turns to the work at hand. And yet he keeps thinking about her life choices. Maybe she sees something he cannot. He thinks of a story his mother used to tell him as a boy about six blind men and their encounter with an elephant. The first man approaches the elephant and grabs hold of one of the animal's legs. 'Ah, the elephant is a tree, this is the trunk,' he says.

The next blind man goes round the back and takes hold of the tail. 'You fool, the elephant is a kind of rope.'

The third blind man stretches out his hands and feels the trunk. 'You're both wrong. The elephant is a type of snake.'

The fourth man reaches for the tusks. 'What nonsense. The elephant is a kind of spear.'

The fifth man grabs the elephant's ear. 'No, no, the elephant is a type of fan for when the weather gets hot.'

Finally, the last blind man approaches the belly. 'You are all wrong. The elephant is a wall.'

The six blind men turn to the elephant keeper.

'Which of us is right?' they ask.

'You are all right, and you are all wrong,' says the elephant keeper.

We're both blind, the doctor's wife and I, PK reflects. We only see and understand what is right in front of us.

The next morning, he starts out west again. He has the address of the rich man's friend, also a doctor, who lives in Delaram, halfway to Herat.

This friend receives him warmly at the city border, invites him to his home and offers him tea. As they sit drinking, the doctor reaches under his bed.

'Do you want a look?' asks the doctor, still a bachelor, and passes PK a bundle of American *Playboy* magazines.

PK flips through them and gives them back. No wonder Afghan men have to resort to these kinds of magazines when all the women in their country are hidden from view. The bare breasts are like the pieces of an elephant's body, he thinks. Surely the young doctor would be more satisfied with a real woman?

He can feel the tiredness come, the nagging headache, the aching in his thigh muscles. He sips his tea and stares outside. But instead of Afghanistan, he sees his village by the river at the edge of the forest. The images still live in his memory.

The next day, he cycles on under a tall sky, a chill caressing his cheeks, his mind empty of thoughts.

Delaram – Herat – Islam Qala

After Delaram, the East–West A1 turns north towards Herat. This is the route everyone takes, and therefore the route PK takes. There is no real alternative. It is the main road for hippies and locals alike.

PK rides from dawn to dusk with just an hour's break for lunch. The same light grey concrete slabs with the irritating joins between them. The bike jumps with each seam. Not something the Russians thought about when they built the road, clearly. What was wrong with asphalt?

He does not worry too much about where he will sleep. Something always turns up. But of the hundreds of addresses in his notebook, none of them can be found along this road. The majority are in Europe. Yet, the people of rural Afghanistan are extremely hospitable, he is discovering. They invite him in for tea and food, and often offer him a bed to sleep in. Of course they can provide shelter for the night. He is welcomed without reservation. He does not even have to draw in exchange for something to eat.

He keeps pedalling, his eyes fixed on the horizon. He is overtaken by trucks loaded with hay, mattresses and goats heading west, and once or twice a day he meets an imaginatively painted bus full of Europeans heading east. He knows that most of them will be sitting in the cafés of Chicken Street within a week, and then outside the Indian Coffee House a few weeks after that, sharing tips and experiences from the road.

The budget hostel in Herat is one of the dirtiest he has ever stayed in. He lies in a bed with a base made of braided rope but with no mattress. His sleep is fitful and broken by nightmares. Horrible nightmares. Beggars approach him in groups, ten, twenty, thirty of them. Hands outstretched. He looks down at their calloused palms, raises his eyes and sees they have no heads. An army of headless beggars, closing in on him. Their demands are a hoarse whisper, but he can hear their threats clearly nonetheless.

The next morning, he wakes to the sun shining through a small opening above his head. He is sweaty and dirty; he has not washed in days. His body is sticky. His mouth is dry. The floor is gravelly and the painted concrete floor is flaking. *Rudolf was murdered in this bed*, has been rather ominously scrawled on the wall beside him. Who was Rudolf, how was he murdered, and by whom? His dreams are echoes of the images of famine and suffering he used to paint when he lived under the bridges of New Delhi.

The day is beginning, and he heads out onto the streets of Herat to make some money. He wants to add to the thick wad of notes stuffed into the cloth bag that hangs around his neck and in the hidden pockets sewn into his trousers. Then he will eat his fill and continue on west. Only once his pockets and stomach are satisfied will he think of Lotta.

But less than one hundred metres from the hotel, a car stops in front of him and a man jumps out from the passenger seat. He introduces himself and explains that he is an adviser to the district governor.

'Get in the car, please,' he says.

'Okay,' PK says.

'The governor has a PhD in political science, he is a very important and intelligent man,' explains the adviser in the back seat of the car as it zooms through Herat's narrow streets.

'We have noticed that you are offering your services as an artist. The governor wants a portrait.'

The governor lives in a grand house protected by fences and guards at the front entrance. PK greets the governor, who is waiting for them. He examines PK, squints. PK knows what this means. They sit down in the courtyard and PK works quickly. Before long his concentrated pencil marks have conjured away the squint. The governor is delighted.

'The best portrait I have ever seen,' he exclaims, and then asks if there is anything he can do for the Indian artist.

PK tells him his Afghan visa expired two weeks ago and that he will have problems when he reaches the border with Iran.

'No, you won't,' the governor replies confidently.

'No?'

'I will take care of it.'

Indeed, when PK shows the border police at Islam Qala his passport and the expired visa inside, they merely smile and wave him on.

Islam Qala – Taybad – Farhadgerd – Mashhad – Bojnurd – Azadshahr – Sari – Amol – Tehran

In Iran, he suffers setbacks. He sleeps for two nights by the side of the road, with nothing more than fruit in his belly. He has money in the cloth bag around his neck – that is not the problem – but he is too far from civilization to buy anything. From the border, he hitchhikes with a truck, but is dropped again after an hour. He continues to cycle, but he has ridden more days in a row than he really has the energy for, and his legs and bottom are so sore he can barely sit down in the saddle. He feels his ribs and knows he has lost weight. When he looks at his reflection, he sees a hippy staring back at him.

He decides to rest in a white beach pavilion in the small resort town of Sari, on the Caspian Sea. They sell ice cream here during the day, he thinks. Now it is night, the beach is deserted. He rolls out a sleeping bag, settles himself gently on the floor, careful not to hurt his backside. His stomach aches from hunger. He falls into an exhausted state half-way between wakefulness and sleep. The beach is so light, the sea so calm, the sky so blue. It is a beautiful place to drift away.

Every time he has sunk this far, been this close to rock bottom, something has happened to pull him back up again. As the sun rises over the pavilion the next morning, he rouses gently from his torpor. He would happily never open his eyes again. That is his first thought. He wants to remain on the edge a while longer, then plunge into the dreamless sleep of eternal darkness.

Just then, he hears laughter. He is woken properly and

opens his eyes. He is surrounded by ten girls lifting their veils and smiling at him. Such pleasant expressions on their sweet Persian faces, he thinks. They look as if they want to eat him. He sits up and reflexively reaches for his sketchbook to show them his drawings. It's the best way to communicate. It usually works.

But one of them speaks English.

'I'm an artist,' PK says.

They are not figments of his famished imagination. The girl tells him they are students from Tehran who have come to spend the day by the beach. They have brought a picnic. He flips through the sketchbook and tells them about his journey from India. They laugh and ply him with food. Bread, yogurt, dates and olives. Such a sweet feeling as they line his stomach.

He has ridden all the way from India, via Afghanistan's snow-topped mountains and through the Shah's Promised Land, on his way to Europe and the woman he loves. A murmur runs through his audience.

'How wonderful!' exclaims the English-speaking girl.

They give him food to pack in his backpack.

If there is one thing he has learned about life, it is that sometimes it pays to come close to the abyss.

After Sari, he feels lighter on his bike again. The villages arrive faster, he meets more people and is often invited into people's homes for food and shelter. Some Iranians are disparaging about the shoddy bike he bought in Afghanistan, so he buys a new one in a market he passes on the way.

Refreshed, excited, carrying a full bottle of water and with a newly oiled bike chain, he continues along Highway 79 towards Tehran, where he hopes a letter from Lotta will be waiting.

The spring sun warms his thighs during the afternoon while the evening chills his cheeks after dusk. He stops at teahouses, drinks and draws the other guests, and is thus invited home. He has not stayed one night in a hotel since Herat in Afghanistan.

Before he goes to sleep he thinks of Lotta. He is still confident she will welcome him with open arms. It has not occurred to him yet that she might have changed her mind or met another man. He is so convinced of the steadfastness of their love that doubt does not have a chance.

There was nothing keeping him in India now his mother was gone. Sure, he still had his father and brothers and sister in Orissa, and all his friends from art school and the Congress Party in Delhi, but he has only ever really loved his mother. And now Lotta. He cannot travel to Kalabati. Lotta, however, is waiting for him just beyond the horizon.

His mind obsesses over one thought for hours as he rides: he must be reunited with Lotta. It is either that or die. And this idea wipes away all fear. Whatever will be will be, it's best if I don't overthink it, he philosophizes as he pedals past villages and towns with names like Qaemshahr, Shirgah and Pol-e-Sefid.

He is being driven by emotion not rational thought, he knows that. He is listening to his heart, his gut. A bicycle trip this long is foolish. The dangers are many, the risk of major setbacks constant. Perhaps the plan is downright impossible. But it is only by refusing to think logically that he can continue on.

And yet so far no one he has met has told him the trip to Sweden is foolish. In fact, when PK tells people he is riding to Scandinavia, they react as if it is perfectly normal. The route is full of romantics like him. Tireless travellers. Cultural refugees. Seekers. Besides all the hippies, he also meets migrants; poor Asians on the way to wealthy Europe. With these companions, he shares the feeling that anything is possible.

Back in India, he was met with a different reaction. His

friends warned him not to undertake the journey. It's impossible, they said. Bicycles are for poor people. Bicycles are dangerous. Bicycles are slow. You can't. You'll never make it. You're going to die.

But how wrong they were.

So far he has not met a single unfriendly person. He has been lulled into a sense that everyone along the hippy trail is curious, positive, generous and kind. Maybe he could live his whole life in motion, he thinks, every day made up of first encounters with interesting people.

In Iran the hospitality continues. He sleeps less and less outside and after leaving the Caspian Sea, he is almost never alone or hungry. He receives water, dried fish, apples, oranges and dates along the way. He sleeps every night in a bed without having to pay a single rial. His ticket to the bountiful Promised Land is the fact that he is Indian.

'Oh, India,' they say. 'A very good country.'

'You think so?'

Until his recent death, the Indian President was a Muslim by the name of Fakhruddin Ali Ahmed. Iranian newspapers devoted pages to his obituary, the Muslim who reached the top in a Hindu country.

People repeat the same speech he has heard so many times since he crossed the border. So generous of the Hindus to make a Muslim president, they say. PK does not see it in terms of generosity. In truth, it was a way to appease the country's minorities, a clever gesture that involved no real sacrifice. The office of president was largely meaningless; the Prime Minister was really the one in charge.

But the Iranians are impressed nevertheless. Muslims in PK's country have the same rights as everyone else, they say. And yes, it is true, on paper at least. An old man tells him about the historian al-Biruni who travelled from Persia to India a thousand years ago. The Hindus told him

India was the most perfect country, with the most powerful kings, the finest religion and the most advanced science. To this old man, India shimmered in gold and silver.

Even if that was the case back then, the India of today is no paradise on earth, PK thinks to himself. The capital's slums reek. But he does not say so. He makes no objection. It is easier that way. He does not want to disappoint his hosts. Such illusions are the basis for an easy friendship.

In contrast, everything about Iran is rich and orderly; the change was noticeable as soon as he crossed the border. The Afghan border guards were dressed in dirty, worn uniforms, their border stations dilapidated. On the Iranian side, everything is new and clean, the people are better dressed and look healthier, the cars are modern, roadside stops are equipped with luxurious sofas and vending machines delivering cold, clean water for free. A border can make all the difference.

He rides west along the Caspian Sea and then south towards Tehran. Another, more southerly, road is actually closer, but the hippy buses usually take this one, and he does not dare deviate. As long as he stays on the hippy trail, he will meet other travellers whom he can draw, and therefore continue to make money. They are also generous with their advice and offer assistance when he gets into trouble.

He needs rest. By now he has taken on the appearance of a wandering holy man, his hair is matted and his body smeared with dirt. He rents a tent at a camping ground outside Mashhad and unpacks everything he has, peels off his filthy clothes and scrubs them with a bar of soap. He shaves, trims his nasal hair, lathers up and lets the hot water wash over him. It has been a long time since he felt this clean.

A small lake occupies the middle of the campsite, alongside the grave of a famous Iranian poet. A mosque sits nestled on an island in the middle of the water, illuminated by coloured lights once dusk falls. In the evenings, people come from the city to enjoy the tranquillity and visit these sites of pilgrimage. They bring food and blankets and picnic until late.

PK understands that this is a golden opportunity. He sets up his easel and gets his sign translated into Persian. Then he sits and waits.

By the first day, a queue has already formed. He draws all evening and the next, earning himself good money. Iranians are rich. PK notices they arrive in big, expensive cars.

He puts no price on his sign. When people ask how much, he answers only, 'Whatever you think it's worth.'

Iranians gladly pay five, sometimes even ten times more for a portrait than he is accustomed to, in addition to giving him food, fruit, tea and rose water.

Iran has been so welcoming, but now his thoughts turn to the road ahead, and Europe. He has heard so many warnings that doubt has begun to creep in; he worries that things might not continue as smoothly once he makes it out of Asia and into this new continent.

Tehran – Qazvin

But first comes Tehran, and it's chaos. Cars are everywhere, jostling for space in the narrow streets with trucks, buses, carts loaded with goods, as well as cyclists trying not to get crushed, their faces wrapped in shawls to avoid swallowing too much dust and grit.

PK adjusts his backside on the saddle and continues pedalling hard, signalling several times with an extra large horn that he has mounted on the handlebar to make himself heard in the traffic. The horn emits a loud, penetrating sound. He notices how the motorcyclists turn their heads to see who, or what, is making the noise. It is his only weapon against the thundering trucks.

Despite the cacophony around him, he is reflecting on the person he has become, who he used to be and the person he might turn into once he arrives in Sweden. He pedals to shut out any other thoughts.

He is a hybrid. Sometimes he thinks all cultures and beliefs coexist inside him.

He is one of India's oppressed indigenous people, a symbol for the injustices of the caste system, and at the same time a man on his way out into the world. He is a poor village boy and a successful city man. He owns nothing and everything at once. He is knowledgeable about art history, romanticism and the colours of Turner's English landscapes, and yet he hardly knows where Sweden is. Already, he has had a more eventful life than he ever dreamed possible as a child, yet he still feels inexperienced, believes literally what people tell him and is curious to learn new things. He has attempted suicide three times, almost starved to death, and yet he is a lighthearted and, dare he say it, happy human being. He believes in destiny and tradition, but also in the liberty that comes from rejecting such ideas.

I am a chameleon. I can blend in anywhere. I can be an outcast among outcasts, important among important people.

But he knows his limitations. He has never demanded to be noticed, he does not know how to affect others or his surroundings.

In Tehran, he acquires a white piece of cardboard that he secures via a wooden stick to his luggage carrier. On it, he writes, *I am an Indian artist on my way to Sweden.* He attaches his portfolio as well, including everything he has done since he left Kabul. Now, he is a rolling advertisement for himself.

As he rides through Tehran, he notices another portrait, this time not by him. Wherever he goes, on lamp posts and the façades of houses, hangs the same picture.

'Who's that?' he asks eventually, pointing to the ubiquitous young man.

'The son of the King of Kings,' people tell him. 'The Prince of Princes.'

The King of Kings? The Prince of Princes?

'Don't you know who the Shah is?' says a fruit seller. 'The Shah of Iran? That's his son. One day he will take over,' says the man, pointing to the portrait.

He likes it. The young man looks friendly. He makes a drawing of the Prince of Princes and fastens it to the placard that has become a sail on the back of his bike.

The drawing attracts attention. A queue develops in one of Tehran's squares as people watch him work and wait to be drawn themselves.

He cycles out of the Iranian capital, and heads west along Highway 2 towards Tabriz. Someone tells him he has cycled over three thousand kilometres since his start in New Delhi. He never thinks in kilometres. What can a number tell you about a journey? It means such different things depending on your method of transportation, whether on a plane, a bus or a bike. He has been going for almost two months, and he must have at least as long ahead of him. This has more meaning than three thousand kilometres.

The sun is hot without burning his skin and the wind fans him without slowing him down. A good day for cycling. The question, as always, is where is he going to sleep tonight? But he is not worried. It is one of the uncertainties he has learned to live with, and even appreciate. He has slept in tents, gazebos and among cattle in their sheds. The standard of his accommodation has varied, but it has always been sufficient for his needs.

Either he collapses, or reaches his goal. Arrive or die trying. Had his mother still been alive, it would have been different. She was the love that could have kept him in India. But now he is leaving all that ridiculousness behind. He presses on, trying to resurrect the feeling Lotta gave him back in India, that life is not meaningless.

But what if she has changed her mind? What if she no longer wants him?

Qazvin – Zanjan – Tabriz

As PK pedals through Iran, news has spread back home in Orissa about his big trip west. He has been sending regular excerpts from his diary to a local news-paper, and they are published unedited. His older brother sends PK the newspaper clippings, and tells everyone he knows about PK's journey. He has become the talk of the entire state.

He may be the furthest he has ever been from home, but he feels utterly present. From this distance, so many thousands of miles from the Brahmins, his untouchability means nothing. Everybody loves success. The Brahmins can only treat you badly as long as you stay in your home village, working in a simple job, making no money. Then their talk of ritual purity carries weight. But when you make a name for yourself, a career, suddenly your low caste melts into insignificance. The higher castes bow to you. Oh, the falsehood, the hypocrisy!

One of the articles he sends from Iran causes a particular stir. His brother writes to say everyone has been talking about it.

The story arises from the most basic of human activi-ties, and goes like this. One day he squats behind a tuft of high dry grass in the Iranian desert and relieves himself. His bicycle with his placards and portfolio is parked on the hard shoulder and looks like a beached sailboat in the distance. The sun is shining and a slight breeze makes the yellow blades of grass sway. As he sits, his mind wanders to an event that occurred when he was no more than six or maybe seven years old. He had gone to the outskirts of the village to find a place to relieve himself. A tree: that looked good. He climbed it. There was nothing strange about that. People did so in thousands of villages all over India; the countryside was the toilet. PK was smart to do his business from a height: that way he could avoid the smell and the flies.

Suddenly, he heard a roar. A roar that indicated surprise as much as anger. Terrified, PK glanced down. Beneath him he saw an old man, and on his head were the contents of PK's bowels. And not just any man. He was a Brahmin. PK jumped down and ran. The Brahmin ran after him, but PK was young and quick and the Brahmin was old and slow and dressed in an unwieldy ankle-length piece of cloth. PK escaped.

Never again did he defecate in the trees.

He looks around, out across the Iranian desert. There is no soul in sight, no risk of contaminating any holy men out here. He sits face to face with the long grass. His friends, he thinks.

'Dear grass,' he begins after checking no one can hear him.

'Here you are, struggling in the heat,' he says to one straw in particular, 'as many of your friends have succumbed from dehydration in the desert.'

The blade of grass answers with a polite tremble.

'You once had a big family, but you are almost the only one left... But you are needed. Without you, the desert would be impossible to live in. Here, even the slightest gust of wind grows into a storm and the sand is like a million needles lodging themselves into your face. You and your few remaining friends fight on, and it is thanks to you that the sand doesn't blow away completely.

'Where I come from, Athmallik in the state of Orissa in India, we have other kinds of grasses. And they are our happiness. Rice, our main staple, is also a type of grass. Your cousin. Did you know that?'

A snap of wind snatches hold of the blade and it bends, as if bowing to his wise words.

'I love you, little grass. You are man's peacemaker and Earth's protector. Without you, there would be chaos.'

But the blade of grass says nothing.

'We humans pull you up by your roots. You are our treasure. We use you to build our houses. But we have no right to hurt you like this. Man has his place, as does the wind, the sand and you, blade of grass; you too have yours.'

He pours a few drops of water from his canteen onto the dry grass as a gesture of his appreciation. The earth trembles in gratitude, he imagines.

He mounts his bicycle and is back on the road, but as he rides he decides to record the conversation and send it home to his brother.

And now it has been published in the newspaper. To think people would enjoy it so much! The people of Orissa must have recognized themselves in his words. Surely everyone has turned philosopher while squatting in the bushes, he thinks. Nature has a soul that deserves respect, or else we humans must face the karmic consequences.

He shakes his head and smiles, and travels on faster than usual towards Tabriz, hoping to find a letter waiting for him there.

Tabriz – Marand – Dogubayazit – Erzurum –
Ankara – Istanbul

He pedals, hitchhikes, daydreams, and with tired legs arrives into Tabriz on his new Iranian cycle, his third since leaving Delhi.

Tabriz, Prophet Zoroaster's birthplace. A letter from Lotta is waiting for him. *My dearest,* she begins. And a letter from Linnea, the Austrian girl who was so badly injured in Afghanistan and whom he took to hospital in Kabul. She has arrived safely back home in Vienna. *My dearest*, she also begins. Only later does he think that perhaps Linnea had been in love with him. Or maybe not. His friends in India almost always wrote in such florid prose. All sugar sweet affection, it was the Indian way. So he thinks nothing of it when Linnea writes:

Dearest PK

Hope you are fine. PK, *my baby*, soon you will come to me in Vienna. I believe you should arrive last week. I was waiting for a long time. I hope you come soon. I think about you a lot and when I do that I feel happy. We will have such a wonderful time together. There is so much I want to show you. Now I finish this letter, but I wait patiently for you to arrive.

Ihr treuer Freund.

Linnea.

He jumps back on his bike and continues towards Turkey.

Iran was vast. So is Turkey. The world is vast. He is very tired of all this cycling now. Where is Europe? Will I be in Borås soon?

More often now, he picks up rides with trucks. It is easy to hitchhike in Turkey.

PK never promised anyone he was going to ride all the way. The trip to Europe was never about proving his physical strength or stamina; it was not some challenge of the body. He promised he would arrive by any means, that was all. Had he enough money, he might have bought a plane ticket. He chose to ride a bike because it was the only option available to him. It was all he could afford. He made a virtue out of necessity. The journey was always going to be difficult and laborious.

He sits next to the driver and his friend, dozing as the landscape slowly changes, thoughts of all that has happened in the past year flickering through his mind. Everything about his life is different now, not just the surrounding geography.

Yes, I have changed.

He was awoken from a slumber in a greater sense: meeting Lotta was the alarm that brought everything into focus. Before her, he had trouble distinguishing his own desires from the wishes of others. It was as if he saw no boundary between what he thought of himself and what others thought of him. But she made him aware of the line between his sense of self and his circumstances.

Now, memories from the time before Lotta are already hazy. Had he ever made a decision for himself, taken ownership of his own choices, before he met her? No, he had allowed himself to float, to be led by others. He had been afraid to be seen and heard, and rarely said what he really thought. He listened and imitated. He had been a guest in other people's lives. Curious, sure, but ultimately submissive.

He has always tried to please others. Lotta used to tell him he was too naïve, almost like a child. But she also liked that about him. 'The fact that you do not feel the need to keep asserting yourself is your strength', she said.

He also takes the occasional bus ride. With his bike on the roof, he settles into his seat at the front. The vehicle jolts into life and starts along the rough, straight road between Van and Ankara.

People spoke good English in Iran, but in Turkey it is impossible to make himself understood. In the absence of words, he draws. Everyone understands the pictures, regardless of their lack of a common tongue. He draws quick caricatures of other passengers. The entire bus bursts into laughter when he reveals the results. The moustached men and scarf-wearing women offer up bread, cheese and fruit. He sits cross-legged, eating sweet apples and plump, bitter olives, and looks out over the plains. They understand each other somehow.

The story is repeated on several buses and in cafés, restaurants and shelters. The Turkish people love to laugh. He receives invitations to their homes, where he draws in return for shelter and something to eat. You are such kind, warm-hearted people, he tells them. They are flattered and ply him with more food.

Once in Istanbul, he gets up early. The minarets are making their supplications as he hurries to the main post office to see if there are any letters waiting for him. One from Lotta with dense rows of her characteristically squiggly handwriting. One from his father. And one from Linnea in Vienna. Hers is thick and has been sent by recorded mail. Out falls a train ticket: the Trans Balkan Express from Istanbul to Vienna.

The Long Journey

* * *

He walks along the Golden Horn and looks out over the blue water and the covered Galata Bridge with all its shops and restaurants. Istanbul smells like Asia, but somehow feels different. He cannot put his finger on what it is exactly. He walks through the streets towards the Topkapi Palace and breathes in the chilly morning air thick with wood smoke, pine and the taste of the sea. Cigarette smoke wafts out of the teahouses. Steamboat horns blast as he climbs up the hills, and at the top he can still hear the muffled sounds of old 1950s American Chevrolets and Buicks cruising along the streets of Istanbul below. The cars are even older than the ones back home. But the women dress in the latest fashions, unlike in Afghanistan and Iran. Blouses, skirts, jeans, and hair worn down around their shoulders. Nowhere does he see them covered by scarves, niqab or any other form of concealment.

He senses that Istanbul is a premonition of his future.

So many domes and bridges, and so solidly built. In school, PK read about Tamerlane, the warlord who razed Delhi and executed large portions of the town's male population. Was he Turkish? He was born near Samarkand, which is now part of the Soviet Union. Anyway, he only had one eye, PK thinks as he sits on a stool near the Blue Mosque, drinking a cold glass of salty ayran.

He stays in a small budget hotel near Sirkeci, the railway station on the European side. There, he feels lonely and sad. He sits on his narrow bed in the eight-bed dorm room and reads his letters over and over again to remind himself that there are people in the world who care about him. He is surrounded by millions of people and yet he is so very small and so very alone. Everyone is on their way somewhere else, but he is stuck, spinning.

He goes to the bank to cash a cheque given as payment for a picture. As he sits behind a desk waiting for the money, he takes out his sketchbook and a pencil – as habit dictates – and starts drawing one of the bankers. After a few minutes, a crowd has gathered around him. The staff stop what they are doing and join the circle.

'It looks just like me!' the banker laughs when he sees the portrait. 'You are very talented, Mr Indian!' and shows it to his colleagues.

One of the women working at the bank would like to have her portrait done too. She is so beautiful and PK wants to capture her face. But he is nervous about drawing women, in case they take offence at the results. Men are more relaxed. No, he does not want to take the risk, they might throw him out. Especially with such a pretty face.

'I'm sorry, I don't have time,' he says, bowing politely.

Eager to get away, PK writes *Best wishes!* in a corner of the portrait, tears the paper from the pad and hands it to the banker. He wants to pay.

'How much?' he asks.

'Whatever you like.' This is PK's standard response these days.

He pays well, enough for PK to afford to eat out every day for at least a week.

Feeling upbeat and flush with cash, he takes a taxi to Istiklal Avenue, a shopping street on the other side of the Bosphorus. He wants to buy a gift for Lotta. While in the taxi, he takes out his sketchbook and draws the driver as the car struggles up one of the city's hills in its lowest gear. It only takes PK a few minutes to complete and he hands the picture to the driver as soon as they reach his destination. The driver's sullen expression suddenly breaks and a smile bursts across his face. PK wonders for a moment if the man might be about to embrace him. Instead the driver refuses payment for the trip and invites PK to his home. PK accepts, because it means he can save a little more money for Europe.

* * *

He wanders around the covered Grand Bazaar, which reminds him of the streets of Old Delhi, with its small shops and shelves crammed with spices, leather, gold and meerschaum pipes. The basic formula for a market, it has been the same since the beginning of time. Part trade, part theatre. Vendors pull and tug at his clothes, just like back home.

He feels safe. The intrusiveness feels familiar.

In Kabul, he bought leather shoes and a handbag for Lotta. Now he purchases a necklace with turquoise stones strung on a leather strap. Then he goes to The Pudding Shop, not a shop selling desserts but a café serving Turkish cuisine. It's the preferred hangout for hippies at the beginning, or the end, of the road between East and West. He sits in the back of the oblong room and rereads the letters from Lotta and Linnea. Then he stares at the train ticket.

At times he has felt as if this journey was going to last for all eternity. Pedal, hitchhike, bus and bike again. The near-death experiences. The muggy heat, the stubborn midday sun. Blisters have come and gone, his buttocks are now permanently numb, and his stomach is almost always crying with hunger. Even his head feels like a steaming, freshly baked sponge. The train ticket is a gift from heaven. The angels have sent it through their messenger on Earth, Linnea, via the international postal service.

He almost cannot believe it is true. He will ride the train to Vienna. The last leg to Europe does not have to be done by bike.

Europe, he thinks. He wonders if he'll ever fit in.

He looks around at essentially the same scene as the Indian Coffee House in Delhi: backpackers, just like him, and a bulletin board full of hastily written notes.

VW van to India, we leave on Friday, one vacancy.

Magic Bus London–Kathmandu. Five vacant seats.

Has anyone found my Pentax Spot Matic?

What should he do with his bicycle? Take it with him on the train? He tucks the ticket inside his waistband and decides to sell the bike and buy a new one in Vienna. He writes in his notebook: *Steady modern men's bicycle for sale, purchased in Tehran. Only twenty dollars!* He tears out the page and pins it to the bulletin board.

Istanbul – Vienna

He gets off the train at Westbahnhof in Vienna. Is this what Europe looks like? Hefty houses, clean streets and neatly dressed people. A reserved calm. But somehow also strained. It is beautiful. A dreamscape. Like stepping out onto a stage in a puppet theatre. Vienna is a storybook.

Linnea's sister Silvia meets him at the station. Linnea, who so longed for PK and wrote such loving letters, left Vienna for India only two days ago. She waited and waited, but finally gave up, says Silvia. PK never came. Perhaps she thought he had turned around and gone back. And her hunger to return to India had overcome her.

Silvia takes him to the family business, Gallery 10, located in the city centre. Silvia's mother greets him, but also wrinkles her nose and pulls him into the bathroom in the back. There, a tall, old-fashioned bathtub on lion's feet awaits. She fills it with steaming water and bath bubbles, tells him to undress and get in. He is shy, but she is insistent, so he strips naked. Only then does he realize how bad he smells, how filthy his clothes are lying on the floor and how wild his beard and hair have grown.

He bathes and thinks of Europe. Its scent of soap. A far cry from Asia's teeming dirt and kaleidoscopic quotidian life. His heart is more uncertain than ever. The damned worry begins to grow inside him again; he feels a long way from home now.

He stays with Silvia and her boyfriend. An artist and his wheelchair-bound wife also live in the same apartment.

Silvia tells PK about Europe. The truths of her own culture. She wants him to develop thick skin, to be prepared, not to be so naïve.

'People aren't as friendly here, not like in Asia. Europeans are individualists and think only of themselves,' she says, adding that kind, gullible people get into trouble in Europe.

'Watch out, Europeans are racists. You can get beaten at any moment just because you have dark skin,' she continues, explaining in detail how he should greet people, initiate conversations and behave.

PK is grateful for her good advice.

She cares about me, he thinks, as Silvia pours her counsel over him.

In just one week, he has learned a lot about the exotic, foreign culture of Europe.

The artist in Silvia's apartment smokes incessantly. He is kind but always drunk and his behaviour is erratic. One moment he is despondent, gloomy, the next he laughs, or is so overtaken by emotion that he pulls PK into his arms. One night he gets up, embraces PK and tells him that he is welcome to kiss his wife.

'Be my guest,' he says.

But PK does not touch her. He does not dare. He does not want to. They do not know each other. They have only ever said hello. Why would he kiss a woman he does not know? Instead, he puts his palms together and bows, a humble gesture to the artist's wheelchair-bound wife, and steps out into the chill of the spring rain.

He walks the glistening, empty streets, along the Danube and towards the lush green of the Town Hall and city parks, thinking about the heat, the dust, the dirt and crowds of Delhi. And the freedom of Europe. It will take some time to get used to it.

In Vienna, he looks up some of the people he met on the hippy trail. His notebook is full of the addresses of fellow travellers who told him to make contact. He drinks tea with them, goes to beer halls with them, draws them. They pay handsomely and his travel funds grow.

Now, he thinks, I'll buy myself a nice, expensive bike with lots of gears and ride the last stretch towards my goal.

'You can't ride to Sweden,' says Silvia.

'Yes, I can,' he insists.

Silvia takes him to the Prater, where they walk under the shade of the horse chestnut trees on Hauptallee and ride the Ferris wheel. They take the metro to drab old cafés and drink coffee with whipped cream, travel by tram to gloomy basement restaurants enveloped in a thick fog of tobacco. They are friendly, these people, but why do they keep warning him about the realities of living in Europe? It is as if the kindness and ease of the trip so far have been replaced by stress, irritation and callousness. In Europe, rules not feelings prevail, he learns from these friends. Europeans are less humane than the rest of the world – is that what they mean? He struggles to comprehend it. Tries to believe them.

'PK,' they say, 'you're a good man, you make people good. But you can't change Europe. In Europe, empathy is dying out. Fear is what drives people, not love.'

Love? If they are so attached to rules and regulations, maybe they cannot believe in love? Did that mean Lotta was not really in love with him?

He understands that Europe is hard. At the same time, here, his ideas come to life. He reflects, problematizes, twists the obvious, complicates. He has been swept on in a current of emotion but now he can feel the momentum slowing, becoming a narrower, slower stream. He has hit the riverbed. And now he is breaking through the surface, gasping in oxygen-rich, rational thoughts.

Maybe Lotta does not want him any more?

He lies in the guest room in Silvia's apartment, sinking

into the overly soft mattress and wrapped in the excessively thick duvet, and is beset with doubts. But somehow he is able to gather his strength to counter them. In the darkness he sees his mother. She is sitting on the floor beside the bed and watching him. She is the counterforce. In the flow of his dark memories, she is the small, bright spot. He falls asleep in her glow.

Before he has time to buy a new bicycle, he meets the gallery owner, who introduces himself as Herr Manfred Scheer and tells PK he admires his determination.

'To make a sacrifice for someone you love is a wonderful and enviable thing. Imagine if more people let themselves be guided by love,' Herr Scheer thinks aloud. 'The world would be a much more beautiful place,' he continues, before telling PK he has something for him.

They go into his office and the man hands PK an oblong envelope. He opens it and takes out a ticket. No, two tickets. Two train tickets.

'It's too much,' PK says, wanting to pay for himself.

The gallery owner refuses, but after some hesitation accepts two of PK's artworks instead.

Wien Westbahnhof–Copenhagen Central

Copenhagen Central–Gothenburg Central

Vienna – Passau

He sits, slumped in the plush seat. The stuffing is so soft it feels as if he has no skeleton and is made only of soft tissue. He spent his childhood sleeping on a straw mat on the floor. In his rented room in New Delhi, he had only a bed with a mattress of thin, braided rope. The second-class carriages had only unreserved seats consisting of wooden benches. His bicycle, a hard, tautly sprung leather saddle; the buses in western Asia, unyielding, shiny padded vinyl seats. He was used to feeling his shoulder blades, tailbone and pelvis. He wants to know where his body ends and things begin. Sinking into something so utterly forgiving, with no resistance, feels unreal.

Why do Europeans wrap their bodies in thick layers of pillows, feather cushions and mattresses? Is it the cold, or because they feel lost? Is it fear? Are they afraid of the hardness of their own bodies?

Wien, Melk, Linz, Wels. European cities have peculiar, monosyllabic names.

He is approaching yet another border. The train brakes, screeches to a halt. A damp smell of cold steel, burnt asbestos and wool affronts his nostrils. The corridor fills with uniformed men.

The interior door is flung open.

'*Reispass, bitte!*'

He holds out his green Indian passport.

The West German border guards flip back and forth through the pages of the exotic document. It is not every day they get to check an Indian passport in Passau.

'*Unmöglich, mein Herr*. We are so sorry. Follow here!' the man says in a mixture of German and English.

PK is forced off the train and follows them to a room on the other side of the platform.

'*Scheisse*,' PK mumbles as he steps down from the train. Silvia taught him this useful word as he was leaving Vienna that morning.

This is it, he thinks. They think he is an illegal immigrant coming to settle in their rich and beautiful country. He is going to take their jobs, steal their girls and be a burden on their society. Except that all he wants is to pass through; he has no interest in West Germany.

They ask him to open his worn bag. Their eyes are hard, their expressions unmoving. They think he is carrying illegal goods. No discussion is to be had; they will lock him up for a few days while they organize his deportation back the thousands of miles he has come. They root around among his dirty clothes and find bicycle tubing and bundles of light blue aerogram letters tied together with a length of thin, grubby rope.

'We will contact the Indian Embassy in West Germany and they will buy a ticket for you so you can go home again,' says one of the officers as he lifts up a blue shirt and holds it at arm's length between his thumb and index finger, as if it were contagious.

PK's grandfather used to say that if you use only two fingers to do your work, the results can only dissatisfy you. Of course, the shirt smelled bad: it had been a long time since he had been able to wash it. But the officer is clearly unhappy with his job; he is on autopilot. Or so his grandfather would have said had he been there.

The officer unfolds a wrinkled newspaper article. It is written in English and has been torn from the Indian magazine *Youth Times*. At least so it says at the top of the page. He starts reading.

'Oh, it says here he's married.'

Eight policemen gather around the brown Indian hippy with the long curly hair and the dirty bag. One of them unfolds one of the blue aerograms and reads. It is written by a woman, he gathers when he looks at the sender. He is satisfied that the Indian and the woman are more than just friends.

'Yes, it seems so. He's married,' says the other man. 'With a Swedish woman,' he adds.

'Her name is Lotta,' says the officer with the newspaper article, who then folds it again.

PK begins to tell the German passport police about his journey's beginning, back in New Delhi, India, his homeland, and the bicycle ride through deserts and over mountains, across seven countries and two continents, all the hundreds of stops along the way to drink, eat and sleep in villages and towns. Despite the incredible hospitality he has encountered, he very nearly did not make it this far, he says. He switched to train travel in Istanbul and there are now only two countries remaining between him and—

'Get to the point,' one of the men interrupts.

'I'm not smuggling drugs and I have no plans to settle in West Germany.'

He sees the scepticism in their eyes and grows despondent. One of the officers says it's time to call the Indian Embassy and arrange transportation. A police car will take him to a detention centre for illegal immigrants or perhaps directly to the airport in Munich for immediate departure. The police explain that West Germany cannot let everyone in who comes knocking on their door. Then he starts conferring in German with one of his colleagues. PK cannot understand, but he feels as if something is squeezing him around the chest. An evil force. He wails, weeps and moans.

'You can't stop me now! You can't possibly be so heart-less!' PK complains in an ever louder falsetto.

Everything is exploding. His voice, his self-confidence, his conviction. He looks out the window and sees the train still standing on the tracks, waiting to continue north towards Munich. The green carriages are enveloped in a grey mist. A light rain is falling and he is cold.

But Europeans are motivated by rules, not cries from the heart.

The adventure has come to an end. Hope is lost. His future is shattered. All the dreams, all the longing, everything he has been fighting for, everything. All in vain!

Up until this moment, he has been convinced that he would reach his destination eventually. Doubts had come but were driven away, faith has pushed him forward on his mad plan. But after the warnings of friends in Vienna, he is no longer so sure. And now: the officers in Passau, at the border station between Austria and West Germany, do not look happy.

'*Ein moment, bitte!*' says one of the officers, looking at him with an equally rehearsed expression, one designed to reveal no emotion or clue as to what he is thinking.

PK tries to appear as newly in love as possible, but suspects the battle is lost. He prepares to take his bag, go to the waiting room and wait for the next train back to Vienna.

The border guards look again at the letters from Lotta and the article from the *Youth Times*. The article is illustrated with a picture of PK, his cheek pressed against Lotta's.

'He's telling the truth. He's married,' one of the border police says.

PK's façade breaks. Tears pour down his cheeks. Weeping, he tells them the story of the fountain, his art, the prophecy, the meeting, the blessing and the bicycle trip.

The officer, whose expression only moments ago had been so hard, so serious, relaxes. Then he laughs and suddenly seems quite cheerful.

'And you're going to Sweden?' he asks with a new tone.

'To my Lotta.'

'Oh well, so it seems,' he says to his colleague and turns to PK again.

'And she lives in Sweden?' he asks for the fifth time.

'In Borås.'

Passau – Munich – Hamburg – Puttgarden – Rodby – Copenhagen – Helsingborg

It has been a month since he left Istanbul and his third bicycle behind him. His friends were worried about him, refused to let him continue his pedalling, and insisted that he should travel the last part of his journey by safer and faster means. There are many things more dangerous than riding a bicycle through Europe. People are so anxious, so pessimistic, he thinks, tucked up inside the cabin as the train rushes northward, to the cold air that blankets the northern hemisphere. How is he going to survive this far north?

But why be discouraged? The border guards let him in, he was not sent home, he had a ticket all the way to Gothenburg. Surely nothing could go wrong now?

Again and again he reminds himself of what he is, where he comes from, and the emotions that have driven him from India. The anger at the priests who threw stones at him and the teacher who refused to let him sit inside the classroom. The bittersweet feeling at the thought of getting his revenge. Frustration at being born untouchable, and therefore worthless.

Without that frustration, he would not be where he is now, sitting on a train on his way to Sweden. Frustration is his driving force. The feelings of worthlessness are the ones that are leading him to happiness. Without that sense of inferiority, he would never have become an artist. Exclusion is the engine that pushes him along the road and beyond his imagination.

As a child, he was always full of questions. When they worshipped cows and threw stones at him, he asked himself how it was possible that a boy was worth less than an ox. Did his veins not pump with the same blood as the Brahmins? When his classmates refused to play with him, he asked himself what would really happen if he touched them. Aside from their shock and anger. Would the world collapse, the sky fall in, the divine cycle of the universe be knocked out of whack?

'The sun is blocked by many dark clouds, but one day the wind will blow them away.' These were his grandfather's words of comfort when he was in his blackest moods.

Grandfather said other things too, but he did not understand all of it. Words of wisdom like 'We come from love, and it is to love we return: that is the meaning of life' were easy enough to understand, but 'We can't know love if we don't know ourselves' was more obscure. He struggled with that one for a long time.

He sits in a German train compartment remembering Grandpa's wise words, and now, finally, he understands. All he meant was that the precondition of love is self-knowledge.

The black clouds disappeared when he met Lotta. What is it, exactly, that happens when you fall in love? Such a powerful force. Forgiveness. She gave me the power to forgive. That was what happened.

On the platform in Copenhagen, he sees a girl and a boy locked in a tight embrace. She is about to board the train, her suitcase stands by her side. The boy is not going with her. They kiss. Long and deep. Oh my God, they are using tongues! No one is stopping them! In India, someone would have shouted at them, pulled them apart.

So this is Europe, he thinks. My future!

The train creaks through the gears at the ferry terminal in Helsingborg. The Norwegian woman sitting diagonally opposite him looks worried, and then suddenly speaks.

'Do you have a return ticket?'

'No,' he replies. 'Why?'

'They won't let you in if you don't.'

The Swedish border police are on their way. He hears them open the door to the next cabin and ask for passports. The Norwegian woman opens her purse, takes out several bills and stuffs them into PK's shirt pocket.

'Three thousand Swedish kronor,' she says simply.

The police enter. He shows his passport. They look at him sceptically.

'Indian citizen?'

'Yes.'

'And you're visiting Sweden?'

'Is there a problem, sir?'

'What is the purpose of your trip?' the police continue.

'I am married to a Swedish woman.'

Bewildered, the police look at each other as if to determine who is going to have to deal with this mess. One of them asks if he has papers to prove it. PK's heart is cold. They have been blessed by his father, but he does not have one single official document, stamp or signature that actually *says* they are married.

He is at the border, so close now. And yet so far away.

The Norwegian woman gestures to him and points at his shirt pocket. Then he understands. He takes out the wad of notes she thrust upon him and shows them to the police.

Astonishment is followed by a visible relaxation in their demeanour. They smile at each other, back out of the compartment and close the door. PK returns the money to the woman. His own funds have dwindled to almost nothing since leaving Vienna. Most certainly not enough to convince the police to let him in.

'You are an angel,' he says to the woman sitting opposite. He would never have got this far without a whole world full of angels just like her.

* * *

As a child, he had learned to use his creativity to overcome obstacles. His mother used to tell him a story about the crow who could not reach the water in the pot. The bird gathered stones in its beak and dropped them inside, one by one. It took the crow a long time, but eventually it filled the pot with enough gravel to raise the water to a level at which it could drink.

'Think like a crow,' said his mother.

But sometimes obstacles are still insurmountable. If everything had depended upon his own individual means, his ability and talent, he would never have met so many benefactors, the selfless people who helped him on his way. They have been there for him since those days under Minto Bridge in New Delhi, when his stomach ached from hunger and he warmed his cold hands over bonfires of rubbish. Of this he is convinced.

Helsingborg – Gothenburg – Borås

He is cold. Confused and anxious. Expectant. What is he doing here? A bearded Indian, medium height, matted hair, filthy clothes, among all these tall, clean people. The light outside the carriage window dazzles him. A brushstroke of red has been applied across the horizon but the sky is still light, despite the fact that it is the middle of the night. How is that possible?

He falls asleep. By the time he awakes the sun is high and streaming into the compartment. The train is stationary. Sweating, he pulls down the window and leans out. White flowers – a type of anemone, he learns later – line the tracks, and the cheerful song of a black bird with a yellow beak fills his ears. The sound is as beautiful as Lata Mangeshkar's voice, the soundtrack to his youth back home in India.

The train stops at Gothenburg Central.

He breathes in the clean, cool air through his nostrils and steps cautiously out onto the newly resurfaced platform. Everything is so different to all the other cities he has passed through. Nothing like Asia. No sweaty bodies pressing against him. No porters, no bells as the tea sellers pass, and definitely no beggars. But also different from Istanbul and Vienna. No chimneys with sooty black smoke, no minaret cries, no crumbling façades, none of the stench of petrol or coal.

Everything is so quiet, clean and empty. At home in India, he often wondered where all the people came from. How could so many squeeze into one place? Here, however, he asks himself where they have all gone. Hello? Where are you hiding?

On the square in front of the train station, he asks a passer-by for the nearest youth hostel. Then a backpacker whom he met on his way from New Delhi appears. He lives in Gothenburg, and can take him to the Salvation Army Guesthouse. He is grateful for the continued help of the friends he made on the hippy trail.

He stands in the youth hostel's shared bathroom shaving, having just finished his shower. Beside him a white man is also washing, his clothes as dirty as PK's. His skin is scarred and his eyes are bloodshot. Suddenly, he removes his teeth and lifts off his hair. Fear grips hold of PK. He screams. Black magic!

The magician turns and, in broken English, asks why he is screaming.

PK does not answer, but gathers his razor, stuffs it into his toilet bag and runs to the front desk to tell them about the fakir in the bathroom.

'Watch out, he could be dangerous,' he tells the young man on reception. 'Believe me, I'm from India, I know the harm black magic can do.'

'How much have you had to drink exactly?' the receptionist replies.

He finds a payphone and calls Lotta.

'I can't believe it, you're in Gothenburg!' she says.

Fear drowns out any pleasure he feels in finally hearing her voice. He tells her he has just met a magician, but no one believes him. And neither does she apparently. She laughs and asks if PK has ever seen false teeth or a toupee before.

She'll be there soon, very soon, to fetch him.

He is standing by the reception desk of the Salvation Army Guesthouse for young men in Gothenburg, when he sees her. She is wearing a dark blue blazer with gold buttons.

Neither of them speak. It has been sixteen months since they parted at the railway station in New Delhi.

PK has been on the verge of a breakdown, standing there in the lobby waiting for Lotta. The last few days have been exhausting. But all tiredness is gone, obliterated by the rush of anticipation pumping through his body.

He shakes himself, tries to give words to his feelings, but nothing makes sense. He looks at her. And starts to cry.

Lotta knows that he is often overcome by the power of his emotions. So she suggests they take a walk. To the Garden Society, she says.

'A café in the midst of flowers.'

They stop for coffee. The sun is big, the air is warm. The sky a crisp light blue. The wood anemones are in flower all along the canal.

So big this year! Lotta is thinking. She has never seen such large anemones. As big as Ferris wheels! she says to herself as they walk hand in hand. PK has no idea what size wood anemones usually are, and anyway, his mind is somewhere else.

PK looks down at the canal and marvels at the clarity of the water. Not at all black and viscous.

They ride the very last bit of his journey together, in her yellow car, past places he cannot pronounce.

Landvetter, Bollebygd, Sandared, Sjömarken.

Suddenly, fear surges through him again. That she might have changed her mind, that her father might disapprove, that he might not fit in.

But they are already on their way to Borås.

He is approaching his final stop. It must have been pre-determined. It must be fate. His fate.

28 May 1977. Finally, he is home.

Homecoming

The apartment with the pink plaster façade on Ulvensgatan consists of three rooms and belongs to Lotta's family. Her mother and father live in another apartment on the floor above. It is PK's first summer in Sweden. He spends most of it in a knitted turtleneck and a wool jacket, sitting on a wooden chair in the living room with the window open, listening to the singing of birds and the rustling of birch trees. Now and then a car drives past. Borås is a world away from the cities he had cycled through, where you had to concentrate to distinguish individual sounds in the thundering cacophony of rumbling and screeching.

He likes the silence: it gives him a sense of peace. But sometimes it is too much of a good thing, and he shudders. Everyone on the bus, for example, looks away. When he ventures a few words to his fellow passengers they answer politely, cordially even. But no one initiates contact. They sit shoulder to shoulder, and yet each is encased in his own refrigerator, always cold.

Sometimes it feels like he has passed into another world altogether, away from all the suffering. It is as if this is a reward for his devoted struggle out in the real world. Sweden is emotionally cool and physically comfortable at the same time. It makes his skin itch.

But he will get used to it.

Outside the open window, he sees two men run past in the direction of the forest. They are in a hurry. Danger, he senses. PK rushes outside and follows them into the woods. A fire, he thinks, and these men are going to extinguish it. They can use the water from the nearby lake, soon they'll be passing buckets to each other. They need help.

But there is no smoke. He sees no flames between the trees, no panic in the two men's faces. Dressed in blue tracksuits, they have stopped and are talking calmly to each other, their hands against two nearby tree trunks as if trying to push them over.

PK stares at them.

'What are you doing?' he asks in English.

'Stretching,' they respond.

'Why?'

'We are orienteering.'

PK doesn't know what that means.

'We orienteer.'

PK has no compass to guide him through this strange new world.

There is another man in Sweden. He has not cycled several thousand kilometres over mountains and through deserts, nor was he told as a baby that he will marry a musical woman born under the sign of Taurus. But he always has enough to eat, never sleeps under bridges, and certainly never thinks of suicide. Nor has he drawn portraits of presidents and prime ministers. But he is blond, fair-skinned and Swedish, looks neat and friendly, plays the flute, speaks perfect Swedish, and never misunderstands what is going on around him. And he knows Lotta very well. They have been singing in the same choir for years.

His name is Bengt. It is much easier to pronounce than Pradyumna Kumar.

One evening Bengt comes to visit. He talks and talks, studying PK and Lotta as they sit beside each other on the couch. His speech is rushed and his looks are strange. PK begins to wonder if he is unwell.

Hours pass, evening turns to night, but Bengt refuses to go home.

'Why is he staying so long?' PK asks Lotta as the clock turns three and Bengt is in the bathroom.

In the end PK is too tired to stay up any longer, trying to follow their guest's monologue in Swedish. He goes out and takes a walk, thinking it might encourage Bengt to go home.

But when PK returns Bengt is still there, his eyes red and puffy, his cheeks stained with tears. Suddenly their guest rises to his feet, slams the door and disappears down the stairs. Finally, they are alone. PK hears the main door slam again. Then all is quiet.

'Why was he crying?' PK asks.

'We've known each other a long time,' Lotta begins,

'we're friends, nothing more. But I realize now that he's in love with me. He can't take it that you're here, living with me.' Bengt thinks PK is a nice man, but that he should not be staying with Lotta.

PK lies down in bed next to Lotta and watches the shadows from the street dance on the ceiling. But sleep is impossible. His mind is spinning, obsessing on the same thought: *There should be two Lottas, one for me and one for Bengt.*

The next morning he gets up and announces that he is going to the bicycle shop.

'Why?'

'I want to buy a bike.'

She looks at him, puzzled.

'A good, sturdy bike that can take me all the way back to India.'

Lotta starts to cry, and PK leaves.

PK can think of nothing but Bengt for the rest of the day. It pains PK to think that he would be a perfect match for Lotta. He chooses a bicycle and tells the owner he will return the next day to pick it up. On his way back to Lotta's apartment, he bumps into many of his new Swedish friends. 'I'm going to ride home to India,' he tells them. They laugh. But PK is serious, they quickly realize. They have nothing to say to this.

'What am I doing here if there is no love?' PK demands.

The return journey would go faster. This time, he would take the more direct route. He will not stop and hang out on the hippy trail. No, he will ride all day, from morning to nightfall, straight for New Delhi and the India Post main office to see if the job is still available. If that fails, he will take the bus into the Himalayas, find a Buddhist monastery tucked away in some remote and beautiful location, and become a monk.

He wants a home. He does not care about the house, the furnishings or the way it looks. It is security he needs, a place to build a life.

The following night, Lotta and PK are sitting at home on the couch.

'I haven't changed my mind,' he is saying. 'I'm going to ride back to New Delhi.'

Tears continue down Lotta's cheeks.

'Why are you crying?'

'Because I don't want you to buy a bicycle and leave.' She leans closer, hugs him. He lets her. Maybe it is a farewell.

'Should I go now?'

'No, I don't want you to go,' Lotta sniffs. 'I don't care about Bengt. I didn't even know he was in love with me. I want to be with you, together in one big mess. For life.'

Sweden is a strange country. People go around thanking each other for nothing. Not to mention the constant meaningless phrases, like 'What nice weather we're having.' Why bother saying it? All you have to do is look up at the sky to see for yourself if the weather is good or not.

'If your friends and relatives went to Orissa,' he says to Lotta, 'and walked around the main street of my village saying things like "What nice weather we're having, Mr Pravat," people would shake their heads and keep walking. They'd think the foreigners had gone mad.'

But he will probably get used to it.

He is more in tune with social protocol when he meets Lotta's mother for the first time. At least he thinks he is. All he has to do is greet her with the polite phrases in Swedish Lotta has nagged him about.

Ask how she's feeling, then talk about the weather. How are you? Beautiful weather we're having today! he repeats to himself under his breath as the doorbell rings.

But it is cold outside, so he will have to make a change to his speech: How are you? It's cold today! Really cold! Something like that.

Standing eye to eye with his mother-in-law, the moment has arrived.

'How are you?' he begins, and then, 'Very old.'

It's almost right, but not quite. On top of this, his mother-in-law's hearing is bad. She says nothing in return. She must be a melancholy soul, PK thinks.

But later that evening, Lotta is not pleased with his performance. 'Why did you call my mother old? She was very upset.'

'It was a misunderstanding,' he tries to explain.

The meeting with Lotta's father does not go much better.

PK drops onto his knees to touch the old man's feet. That is how you show respect to your elders in India. But apparently not in Sweden. 'Where did the little Indian go?' Lotta's father says later, when describing the meeting.

And then there are the cows. During his first summer in Sweden, they go to visit the family summerhouse in the nearby countryside. That's when PK sees them, out in their pasture. Someone's forgotten to open the gate, PK thinks. Cows should roam free. So he opens it. Before long, the animals have strolled out and into the road.

Cars start honking irritably. PK waves cheerfully back. That is how you get the cows to move out of the way in India too! It turns out they're not so different here after all.

But the farmer is furious.

'Who let the cows out?' he demands in a temper.

'That was *me*,' PK replies proudly.

He takes a four-month course in Swedish for immigrants and works hard at fitting into his new home country. He is used to going everywhere barefoot and sometimes forgets to put on his shoes when he goes outside, even though it is winter. Often it takes the feeling of icy slush between his toes to make him realize his mistake.

A temporary teaching position in the art department of a local high school opens up and PK applies, even though his Swedish is still rudimentary. But art needs no language, everyone understands a picture, he reflects. He receives an invitation to attend an interview at the municipal department of education. He wears shoes and brushes his hair. So civilized, so Swedish. Almost.

The red light flashes to green and he enters the interview room, still trying to slow his breathing to mask his anxiety. The interviewer is pacing back and forth, his thumbs hooked in his braces. He rocks on his toes, but says nothing. PK's nerves intensify. He does not understand what the man is doing or what it means.

Then, suddenly, the interviewer speaks.

'And what have you *sysslat* with?'

He has learned the Swedish word for work, *arbeta*, and even *jobba*, but he has never heard this word *sysslat* before. Later he would learn it meant 'to be occupied'. The Swedish Employment Service's favourite term; it is not a job, it is an 'occupation', you do not work, you are 'occupied with your career'.

The first Swedish person PK had ever met was Jan Lindblad, the famous director of wildlife films. He came to PK's home village in the jungle in 1968 to film the animals of Tikarpada Wildlife Reserve. The teenaged PK served as a runner for the crew and watched in fascination as they dragged their heavy equipment through the undergrowth, rigged up their cameras and connected their devices with long electrical vines.

Jan Lindblad liked PK and called him Jungle Boy. He was so funny and friendly and he treated the untouchables as if they were just like everyone else.

PK observed as Jan Lindblad crept through the vegetation, whistling to attract birds. He was very good at it. He produced melodies and mimicked the animals so that PK laughed until his stomach ached.

That is it! PK realizes in the middle of his interview. The man is asking if PK can whistle. That makes sense! Clearly whistling is a very important skill in Sweden. Teachers whistle to the children to call them in from their break, after all. That is how they do things here in Sweden.

PK takes a deep yogic breath and begins whistling, producing a strong and full sound. I too can be like Jan Lindblad, I too can be Swedish, PK thinks. This will prove I am qualified to teach art in a local school.

But the man does not look happy. He freezes, then raises his palm. Later, PK would learn this was a signal meaning 'stop'. But right now, PK has no idea. In India, a raised palm means 'Great, keep it up!' So he continues, louder and with even greater gusto.

He whistles until his cheeks hurt and then stops. That should be enough.

The interviewer looks away. Then he looks straight into PK's eyes and asks ten short questions about his education and background. Nothing more. Then he goes to the door and opens it. PK gathers his papers.

'Thank you, goodbye!' the man says firmly.

He sounds almost angry.

After the interview, PK tortures himself with questions about the man's behaviour. Why had he been so abrupt? Was he not good enough for the job? Did he whistle the wrong tune?

Yet a few days later, PK receives a call from the head-master of Engelbrecht School. Would Pradyumna Kumar Mahanandia be willing to take a temporary job as an art teacher and report to work early the next morning?

People think their love will never last. He will find it too hard to adapt. The darkness, the cold, the growing racism, even the way Swedes socialize, it will all break him sooner or later, they say. 'Oh God, how can an Indian village boy learn to live in modern Sweden?' they whisper to each other, shaking their heads. 'Before long he will realize just how different it is here and go back to the jungle.'

But PK never longs to return to India. 'Mentally, I have escaped India entirely,' he writes in the red and black diary Lotta has given him. He fills it quickly – and then another, and another – with musings about his new life in Sweden. For the first year he spends his evenings on the couch in the apartment on Ulvensgatan and writes down all his disappointments, new experiences, the people who believe in them and those who do not. He writes as the autumn rain splashes against the façade of the apartment building, as the shards of ice glisten in the winter sun and the blackbirds sing through the open window in the first warmth of the following spring. He lets himself absorb it all, and processes his thoughts in these pages. Sweden and the culture shock have made him a more reflective man.

With every passing day he becomes more Swedish and less Indian. But Lotta is taking an opposite path. She immerses herself in yoga and meditation. She recites mantras as the first rays of morning sun light the sky. PK hates mantras. The monotonous purr reminds him of all that he has escaped: the power of the Brahmins, the alienation and the suicide attempts. But he learns to overcome even those feelings, which still sometimes manifest themselves in physical nausea. He must mute the memories and live with them.

Other aspects of Indian culture he recalls with more fondness, so long as they have nothing to do with religion.

After first arriving, PK painted postcards and posters with Indian motifs, which he sold to friends and colleagues. He had pictures published in several Swedish newspapers. His proudest moment was when the culture section of one of Sweden's biggest newspapers, *Aftonbladet,* published a full-length feature about his art and organized an exhibition of his drawings in its newsroom, just as *The Kabul Times* had done previously. The *Aftonbladet* article led to more shows in the capital.

It is difficult to escape his place of origin, however. People keep telling him to teach yoga, despite his protests that he barely knows enough about it to practise himself, let alone teach. And yet, expectations are high. Offers to lead courses become ever more frequent.

'I've never even taken a yoga class, all I know was taught to me by my big brother,' PK tells the residents of Borås.

'So much the better,' they answer.

When the local community college advertises the city's first ever yoga course taught by a real Indian, places are snapped up fast. Nearly all his students are female.

PK goes through the movements his brother had shown him. It's not much, he thinks. But they seem happy, asking him questions about yoga's deeper philosophical meaning and significance, things Lotta ought to have answered, because he does not really know the answers. And yet, strangely, the women seem satisfied with his confused and partial responses that are neither insightful nor profound, based as they are on fragments he had heard as a young man.

'I smile and teach my yoga classes. At least it's work and earns me money,' PK writes in his diary.

Sometimes his thoughts turn to what would have become of him had he never met Lotta, bought that first bike in New Delhi or started riding west. He daydreams about what life would have been like had he not fallen in love and been charged with the 'energy of forgiveness', and had instead remained in his homeland, an India paralysed by caste conflict. I would have become a politician and fought for the rights of the untouchables, he concludes. Politics would have been my only weapon.

Maybe he would have been elected to Parliament for Indira Gandhi's Congress Party. Then he would have presumably started taking bribes just like everyone else. Power corrupts. That is the way it is. Very few people can resist and remain clean.

Maybe politics would have proved insufficient to quell his anger. Thoughts of revenge had been a feature of his childhood and had even lasted into adulthood. Despite the best efforts of his parents to dissuade and calm him, they have been a part of him ever since he can remember: thoughts of horrific acts of revenge. Until he met Lotta, that is.

'You must forgive,' his mother and father had said.

It has been a long time since PK last thought of revenge. Now, if the anger ever starts to fizz and burn, he understands that the object of his rage is nothing more than a mirror image of himself.

PK wants to be Swedish. He ignores the fact that the people around them remain sceptical. The more friends and colleagues doubt his ability to cope in Sweden, the more he fights to fit in. And it is this struggle to embrace all things Swedish that changes everything. It drives him forward. Learning the language is not easy. He understands most of what is said, but often his pronunciation holds him back. Misunderstandings occur because of misplaced emphasis, a wrong consonant or vowel sound. But each mistake only makes him more determined. He is going to succeed! It is going to work out! As long as he does not give up!

During his first year in Sweden, a teenage student approaches him in the corridor and asks why he has not married an Indian woman instead.

'It would suit you better,' she declares.

'Love knows no borders,' PK responds brusquely and goes out into the schoolyard, where Lotta is waiting for him.

He will overcome these obstacles. He starts teacher training in outdoor education at Mullsjö College outside Jönköping, learns to ski both cross-country and downhill. He takes mountaineering courses in Tarnaby and climbs Sweden's highest peak. He gets a job as a recreational leader at Elfsborg, the largest sports club in Borås, puts on events at the church and for the local chapter of the Red Cross, learns to like cinnamon buns and to ride the family horse. He gains ever more skills and experiences specific to Swedish culture, hoping that eventually Swedes will start treating him as a person and not as a representative of the place where he happened to be born.

Lotta and PK continue living in the apartment in Borås, but every summer they move out to the old family farm at Kroksjöås that used to belong to Lotta's grandparents. There, they grow cauliflowers and potatoes, take walks in the woods and discuss the possibility of eventually moving out to the forest permanently.

Late in the summer of 1985, Emelie is born. Not any old day. 15 August. The same day, thirty-eight years earlier, that India had gained independence from the British. What a coincidence! 'Today I feel freer than ever,' he writes in his diary.

His father, brothers and the rest of the family back home in Orissa see it as an omen.

'Now your roots are firmly planted in your new country,' his father writes in a letter, adding that he hopes PK has not forgotten his Indian ancestry completely. 'I am looking forward to hearing about Emelie's naming ceremony,' he writes.

PK is forced to disguise his aversion to religion. His family in India would be disappointed if he did not organize a *Namkarana* ceremony, the Hindu equivalent of a Christian baptism. Eleven days after their daughter is born, PK and Lotta perform the ritual according to Hindu tradition. They gather the Swedish part of the family – PK's family in India could not afford to come – and they shave the thin tufts of Emelie's hair as PK reads out loud all the auspicious names and honorific titles his father has sent.

'The Swedish side of the family didn't much appreciate the ritual. They looked at Emelie's shaven head as if she was a prisoner in a concentration camp,' he writes in his diary.

But by the time Emelie's brother Karl-Siddhartha is born three years later, they are used to these strange Indian rituals.

After several years of substitute teaching, courses in Swedish for immigrants and further studying, PK sends his transcript from the art school in New Delhi to the Swedish National Board of Education to have it approved. The Swedish authorities accept the qualification and he is now able to take a permanent position as an art teacher at Engelbrecht School.

At the beginning of every semester, he clears away the chairs and benches and tells the students to sit cross-legged on the floor. He wants them to know that as well as being another adult, a responsible, conscientious and composed authority figure, he is also just a kid like them. He imitates jungle birds and animals, lies down on his back and waves his legs in the air. He does headstands, taken from his morning yoga practice in the living room. The children

laugh and understand they need not fear a teacher so willing to make a fool of himself.

The cobra had protected him from the rain as a baby in
the basket in the hut with the broken roof, and it had also
ensured his safe arrival in Borås. Now it continues to protect him in his new country. The students at Engelbrecht
School like to pour sugar into the headmaster and other
teachers' petrol tanks. But PK is spared. No one touch-
es his white Volvo 242. A rumour circulates among the
school's troublemakers that PK keeps a cobra in the boot.

'Never touch the Indian's car, you might get bitten!'

As PK stands in front of his students, his thoughts often
return to his own school days, and all the times in primary
school when he had been bullied by his classmates and the
teacher. The untouchable pariah. Such bullying en masse is
not possible in Sweden, which reassures him.

But it does happen on a smaller scale, even in Borås.
When PK sees Swedish students harassing each other he
bursts with an uncontrollable anger. One of the school's
known bullies makes the mistake of tormenting one of his
victims right before PK's eyes. PK's reaction is instinctive.
He roars. Swedish turns to English and then to Oriya, the
language of his childhood. He is overwhelmed by feelings
difficult to explain to the Swedish kids. He connects to a
deeper anger, rooted in that classroom in Athmallik, and it
explodes right here in his classroom in Sweden.

'Get down on your knees!' he bellows.

A string of Oriya follows, incomprehensible to everyone
but PK.

For the first time, the bully obeys and kneels down, as
he can feel the meaning of PK's words, even if he does
not understand them. The boy bends his head and keeps
his eyes on the floor; he is too scared to move. PK lets his
captive stay there for the rest of the lesson, defeated and
humiliated.

Forcing a student to kneel for more than half an hour is not an acceptable punishment in a Swedish school. PK knows that, but that day, he does not care. The memory of his own vulnerability is still raw. The rage that has been sitting just below the surface for so long takes precedence. He feels ashamed about it afterwards. But many years later, he receives a call from the young bully, now a grown man, drunk and crying. He is ringing to thank PK. A letter follows repeating the sentiment, claiming that his Indian teacher had 'taken the devil out of him'. The victim later tells PK that the experience had also been transformative for him.

'No one ever bullied me again after that; you broke a pattern in a way that everyone else was scared to try,' he said.

Kroksjöås Farm, thirty-five years after the first time he saw a wood anemone. Såken Lake laps against the shore, fir trees rustle in the wind and the laughter of children rolls over the dark surface of the water from the beach on the other side. He loves the sounds of the Scandinavian forest.

He sits on a white garden chair, his feet tickled by the high, yellow grass interspersed with poppies and daisies, and reflects on his life in Sweden. Almost a whole lifetime has passed.

He would not have survived without Lotta.

Now he has taken early retirement to make time to paint. During all those years as a teacher, he found it next to impossible to create anything in the studio tucked into their small apartment in the centre of Borås and then, after they moved to the forest permanently, in the red barn next to the yellow wooden house. Any spare time he once had disappeared entirely when the school started demanding he write long reports for each student using the school's new computer system. It was the perfect excuse to withdraw.

He has already been up for hours, completed his daily yoga practice that, paradoxically, has long been an indispensable part of his morning routine since he was forced to teach it as a newly arrived immigrant. He has had his ginger tea in the conservatory and finally eaten breakfast, a masala omelette on toasted bread. Afternoon is fast approaching in the house by the lake and the children have just woken up.

They are adults now.

Emelie has finished her studies in fashion management with a focus on marketing, and is about to head out into the world of work. She has interned in Copenhagen, rummaged in London's markets, spent a spring in Bombay and has recently been to Orissa to sign contracts with artisans who specialize in weaving ikat scarves.

Karl-Siddhartha, otherwise known as Kid Sid, has been touring Sweden and the rest of Europe as a DJ since he was a teenager. He even won the DMC World DJ Championships at the age of sixteen. He has used the money he has earned to study for a helicopter licence. His dream is to work as a professional helicopter pilot in India, and perhaps fly politicians and businessmen from inaccessible parts of Orissa.

Both children feel a strong attraction to their father's home country.

Their first contact with India was through their cousin Ranjita, who came on a visit to Borås from Athmallik before Emelie and Karl-Siddhartha started school. Emelie thought that their Indian cousin was very strange. Even though she was in her teens, she did not know how to use cutlery. That alone was enough to mark her out as odd to the little Swedes.

The following year PK and Lotta took the children to India for the first time. PK was worried about how it would all go. During his lessons in Swedish for immigrants, he had been taught that children should wear helmets when riding a bicycle. He embraced the Swedish love of safety as if it were written in stone. No more the Indian 'whatever' mentality, from now on it was Swedish helmets, always. Even though they had no plans to ride bikes in India, they packed helmets into their luggage. India is so dangerous, he realized.

Emelie wore a blue styrofoam helmet virtually the whole trip, in small towns as well as large cities, while playing with her cousins in the fields and on dirt paths. The villagers in Athmallik had never seen anything like it.

'Hello, little girl,' they said, laughing and tapping their

fingers on her head. The five-year-old Emelie was furious.

'You never know what could happen,' PK countered when she begged to take it off. It was sweaty and itched.

It is summer and PK is sitting out in the garden by the outhouse they have built for guests, swatting away a stubborn fly. He is trying to formulate his ideas as if explaining them to a Swede who knows nothing about India. Imagine, he will say, that the nobility and clergy occupy all the important positions in society and that you, who belong to neither group, are ostracized wherever you go. Imagine that the people are at first cheerful and open, but quickly frown and turn away as soon as you tell them your name. Imagine that all of Sweden's priests are born to this position, and they stand in front of the churches and yell at you to go away and worship elsewhere. That they will even bend down, gather handfuls of gravel and throw it at you so that you will run, before slamming the door and locking it. And then consider, he continues to his imaginary Swedish friend, these experiences are repeated every day, year after year, even though the law says you have the same rights as everyone else and that it is illegal for you to face such discrimination.

Then he recalls a book he read about in both the Indian and Swedish newspapers that tells the story of an oppressed and exploited low-caste girl called Phoolan Devi who ends up in a criminal gang, becomes a bandit queen and takes bloody revenge on her former tormentors. She was put in prison, but later released and became a Member of Parliament and celebrity all over India, the world even, all because of the book and film made about her life. And yet, in the end, she was murdered by the relatives of her former bullies: revenge by the ones she took revenge upon.

That's what happens if you give an eye for an eye. Continued hatred is the only outcome of a blood feud.

Reprisals prolong suffering. No, revenge is good for no one, PK thinks, breathing in the scent of freshly mown grass.

A gust of wind gently rattles a nearby birch. He looks out over the lake and the ripples shimmering across the water's surface.

PK cannot understand why the government of India does not outlaw the caste system once and for all, relegate it to the history books. Sure, discrimination based on caste is technically illegal. And there are reservations and quotas so that low castes are given a little helping hand. But it is an outright ban that is required. In England, the Church condemned slavery and serfdom as early as 1102, and in Sweden slavery was declared illegal in 1335 by King Magnus Erikson. India's untouchables are not enslaved, but just as serfs in medieval Europe were not allowed into the church, there are still Hindu priests that deny untouchables entry to their temples to this very day. Untouchables are still commonly thought to defile all that is pure and holy.

PK feels the anger swell inside him when he thinks of the injustice. His grandfather, who lived under British colonial rule and attended the Victoria Vernacular School, at least had the dignity of being treated the same as his high-caste schoolmates. But PK, who grew up in the newly liberated and independent India, was forced to sit out on the veranda, to be separated from his classmates and endure the fiercest and subtlest forms of discrimination.

'It was a concerted campaign of oppression, that's what it was,' he mumbles to himself and begins along the path by the lake and up through the pines.

The sun is shining for once over the rain-saturated hamlet. He walks through the drowsy forest, around the mounds of rock and earth wrapped in soft, damp moss. It is as if someone has placed a giant green marzipan blanket over everything, making a traditional Swedish *prinsesstårta,* princess cake, out of nature.

The tall fir trees form a roof over his head. He leaps from stone to stone across a gurgling stream. He emerges on the other side and into a clearing where the dew glistens like silver in the tall grass. A long, slippery footbridge crosses the marshy meadow, and then the trees fold away. There it is, the lake, today smooth and shiny. Dead trunks lie on the sandy beach as if abandoned in a giant game of Mikado. The water is dark brown, almost like Coca-Cola.

'What nice weather we've been having,' PK says as he meets a neighbour on the gravel road that leads back to the cottage.

He thinks about the contradictory feelings that are stirred up inside him every time he returns to his village in India. A few years previously, state politicians in Orissa ordered a helicopter to collect PK, Lotta and their two children and fly them from the state capital to the village where the locals had gathered in what was billed as an official visit. They were to worship PK's resurrection, the successful untouchable boy. To say it had been overwhelming would be an understatement. The Brahmin girls whose fathers had once thrown stones at him kneeled down and touched his feet, before decorating him with garlands of marigolds. But while the Brahmins may now admire him, he was still careful not to challenge their power overtly. Otherwise it could have caused trouble after his return to Sweden.

His older brother Pramod, the one who was a successful railway manager in Bokaro, hired several untouchables to work for him in accordance with the government's edict. And yet, one day, he was found lifeless on the floor of his bungalow. The servant looked down at his face, which had mysteriously grown whiter with each passing year. At the corner of his mouth, a blue foam bubble popped.

'Death by natural causes,' the police said. But his family and friends doubted it.

He had challenged the Brahmins too forcefully, was their conclusion. A law-abiding civil servant who followed the new anti-discrimination laws was still too much for the higher castes. They poisoned him. And the perpetrators, whoever they were, went free.

PK goes down to the shore and skims a flat stone over the smooth surface of the lake. He can physically feel the grief and nausea that come over him every time he smells incense, or hears Hindu temple music, or even prayers or other ritual texts being read aloud in Sanskrit. But in these situations he has a weapon. These feelings are nothing more than passing clouds; before long the wind will blow them on again.

He draws the air into his lungs. It smells of fresh water and reeds. And he listens to the distant splashes and children's laughter from the beach on the other side. The forest makes him calm. The thick tree trunks, pine needles, moss, the heather and stubby blueberry bushes. Our kingdom, for Lotta and me, he thinks.

Autumn arrives and the rain clouds sweep through Borås. PK puts on his rubber boots and goes out into the woods where the rain is streaming down from the towering branches above, causing the moss to swell and glisten. He knows how precarious his memories are. When he thinks of his life in India and the bicycle trip that brought him to Sweden it feels as if it happened to another PK. These days he prefers to stay at home, painting in his studio in the barn, taking walks in the forest, going out with his chainsaw to do some gardening and then returning to their little cottage to look out over the lake.

PK recalls a speech he made only a couple of years ago to Lotta's relatives, the members of the von Schedvin family.

The talk took place in the symbolic heart of the Swedish nobility, Riddarhuset in Stockholm. He was dressed in a dark blue collarless suit and a sand-coloured Indian raw-silk shirt. His moustache was dyed and his hair combed flat.

He had given talks about his life many times before, for study groups and in schools, for civil servants, local associations and pensioner clubs, but here, at the so-called House of the Nobility, he was more nervous than usual. The pompous surroundings, the paintings, the crests and all the fine hand-painted china, it made him feel small and insignificant. But he gathered his courage, stepped up to the microphone and began to talk about his childhood, about the jungle and the elephants, the snakes and the temples, and of course the caste system. He wanted to take this opportunity to make a comparison between the Indian caste system and the Swedish class structure. Priests, warriors, merchants and workers, said the Indians. Nobles, clergy, burghers and peasants, said the Swedes.

Then he told them about the prophecy, his falling in love with Lotta and the bicycle trip to Sweden. Fate, love, his journey.

'I have no power over the direction of my life, and neither do you, dear audience. Look at me! Everything turned out as the prophecy predicted and not how my father, teachers or anyone else planned.'

Yet PK is sure that man has free will, and that destiny is only a framework. The prophets can only predict the contours of a human life. His mother, Kalabati, phrased it in hopeful terms: 'No one is doomed to be untouchable forever and nobody of the highest caste can expect to decide for eternity who can or cannot enter the temples or perform the sacred rituals.'

He went on to explain that laws already existed that made discrimination illegal and quotas were in place to help low castes get an education and jobs, but that India still needed to go further if it wanted to be rid of the caste system.

'A ban! That's my vision.'

More speeches followed. The Utkal University of Culture in Bhubaneswar called and wanted to grant him an honorary doctorate. He could not resist. He was flattered, and proud.

When he was little, they kicked him into the dirt; now they're brushing him down and dressing him with garlands – PK found this amusing. For an untouchable to be granted a doctorate had to mean the world was making some kind of progress, despite all the wars and continued misery.

Once again, he dresses in his dark blue suit, takes a deep breath and steps out onto the stage. The lights are hot, beads of sweat gather on his forehead, and hundreds of pairs of eyes stare back at him. He is given flowers, and an orange cape with a gold fringe is draped over his shoulders. The speech made in his honour is pompous and over-the-top, in good Indian tradition.

'I have not always been so happy in my life as I am now. When I was a young student, I tried many times to end my own life. Every day I struggled to find food to eat and I was always hungry,' PK says when it is his turn.

'Everything starts with the family we grow up in. If the family isn't working, society cannot work.' He continues with one of his grandfather's sayings: with righteousness in your heart, your home will be harmonious, with harmony at home comes order in society, and with order in society comes peace on earth.

And he would not have got this far – to the yellow house in the woods of Sweden – if it had not been for the inspiring example set by the people of Orissa, he adds out of politeness.

'Do not thank me, say thank you to yourselves,' he says, repeating the words of the late Swedish Prime Minister, Olof Palme.

One frostbitten December morning, Lotta, Emelie, Karl-Siddhartha and I board a plane in Gothenburg. We are going to the former kingdom of Athmallik. We fly over Denmark's powder-white fields and Vienna's oxidized copper roofs. We cross over Iran's arid plains and Afghanistan's rocky mountains, where thirty years previously I struggled on my bike in the opposite direction. We pass high above the sun-scorched Ganges plains, where a train once carried me away from the village along gleaming rails, over jungles dark and curly like broccoli, before making a turn at the Bay of Bengal, the Black Pagoda and the temple of the sun god with the magic wheel. Finally, we land in the fields where I grew up.

We rent a car and drive along bumpy roads past the market towns of Dhenkanal and Angul, before turning off the main road down an even narrower track edged by increasingly dense jungle. All the way back to my childhood.

We enter the village to the sound of an orchestra. Eight men walk in front of our four-wheel-drive Chevrolet, which crawls rather than drives for fear of crushing the musicians. I received the same welcome the last time I came to visit, with exactly the same melody, played by the same drums, clarinet, tuba. Villagers line the main street, waving at us as we pass.

We live in the house between the mountains and the river. The house that we built so that we have a place to return to now that both my father and mother are dead and my childhood home is long gone. From here I can coordinate my charitable work: water wells, the school and the activity centre that holds workshops for the women.

I want to help those who have not been as fortunate as myself, even if my work is only a drop in the ocean. There is so much to do. A crowd gathers every morning outside our door, they have come for advice.

We go down to the Mahanadi River, where women wash clothes by the beach, buffaloes and cows wade in the knee-high currents and crocodiles bask on the protruding sandbanks. A procession of men, women and children from the village follows behind us. My personal bodyguard, dressed in a black military-style beret and camouflage, sits beside me, sent and paid for by the state government.

Among the procession is the village bard, a Brahmin who raises his stick to the heavens and shouts his tribute to God, 'Hari Bol!' He laughs, his teeth rattling and red from years of chewing betel nut.

I have two bodyguards then, a Brahmin and a soldier. The best protection a man could hope for.

The Brahmin tells me he has performed this ritual, the laughter and the 'Hari Bol!', every day since 1962 and has not been sick once. God rewards the devout. But Karl-Siddhartha quickly tires of the monotonous chanting and teaches the old man instead to shout out 'Hey you!' in Gothenburg-heavy Swedish.

Halfway to the river, the Brahmin invites us into his home. There, in the darkness, he has erected an altar, as in most Hindu homes. But instead of the usual images of Shiva or Vishnu, he has placed a picture of... Lotta and me.

We stand and watch as the Brahmin falls to his knees, raising his hands to worship the photograph.

I look at Lotta, who shakes her head and smiles. We can hardly believe our eyes.

Postscript

The Indian Caste System

As PK says, the caste system in India is not that hard to understand on the surface. It's when you start to delve more deeply into its divisions and subdivisions that it seems as chaotic and bewildering as a busy Indian street market.

The word caste is derived from the Portuguese *casta*, meaning 'race, breed or ancestry', and originally from the Latin *casto*, meaning 'pure or chaste'. There is no precise translation in Indian languages, but varna and jati are the two most proximate terms. These two concepts represent different levels of social identity within the caste system.

According to Brahminical books like the *Rigveda*, varna in Sanskrit means 'colour, type, or order', inferring the colour of one's skin. Historically there were four main varna existing in a rigid hierarchy. At the top were the Brahmins (teachers, intellectuals, priests), then the Kshatriya (warriors and rulers), followed by the Vaishya (traders, merchants, artisans) and finally the Shudra (labourers, servants).

Some groups of people were banished from the varna system and were referred to as 'untouchables', now known as Dalits. They are socially excluded to this day.

Jati refers to birth and is typically associated with a job

or occupation. The jati belong to one of the four varna, and it's at this point that PK's Western friends throw their hands in the air and change the conversation, because there are thousands of jati. These complex social groups defy clear definition.

The *Rigveda* verses that PK mentions are a collection of ancient Indian Sanskrit hymns dedicated to Rigvedic deities, one of whom is Purusha, the 'cosmic being'. He inhabits everything universally conscious and unconscious and is depicted as a being with a thousand heads, eyes and legs.

The untouchable or Dalit caste to which PK belongs was traditionally involved in occupations that were regarded as impure, such as leatherwork, butchering or removal of animal carcasses, or disposal of rubbish and human waste. They were generally outcasts, banned from everyday social life, physically separated from the rest of the community and forbidden to enter temples or schools. As PK describes, untouchables are social pariahs from the moment of birth, outlawed, vagrant and undesirable, categorized as unpersons by dint of an accident of fate.

Although the Indian caste system has ancient origins, the British Raj exacerbated the problems by making caste organization legally binding, thereby enabling a divide and rule means of government. Between 1860 and 1920, the British segregated Indians by caste, giving the top administrative jobs to the upper castes. However, protests during the 1920s forced the colonial administration to begin a policy of positive discrimination by offering a percentage of government jobs to the lower castes.

The British, on the whole, did not consider untouchables to be subhuman or ritually unclean but useful manpower, and many were recruited into the army. During the Raj rule untouchables were treated with a degree of pragmatic benevolence and they achieved some small emancipation. PK's family did well by the British.

Even so, Mahatma Gandhi started a nationwide movement against untouchability and named the so-called lower classes *Harijan* or 'Children of God'. He started the All-India Anti-Untouchability League and the weekly newspaper *Harijan*. He also undertook a Harijan tour of India between November 1933 and August 1934, which helped spread the message down to the lowest and most oppressed sections of society. However, by renaming untouchables with the seemingly elevated word Harijan, many believed Gandhi papered over the deep-set issue of the persecution of the underclasses. They claimed it only removed 'the offence to the ear' and little else changed. Nowadays Harijan is considered by many to be a derogatory and insulting term. PK himself really dislikes the word, as it can be taken to imply a denial of true parentage.

Untouchables were later called 'Scheduled Castes' and 'Scheduled Tribes' under the India Act of 1935, and the later Indian Constitution of 1950. The constitution also banned discrimination on the basis of caste and announced quotas in government jobs and educational institutions for Scheduled Castes and Tribes. The Untouchability (Offences) Act (1955) provides penalties for discrimination on the grounds that an individual is from a Scheduled Caste.

Despite these measures the divisions between caste groups persist and violence and intolerance continue, especially in rural areas. In the early 21st century, Scheduled Castes or Dalits numbered 170 million people in India.

A recent Human Rights Watch statement says:

> Despite commitments to end caste and descent-based discrimination, the practice persists due to poor enforcement of laws and policies. Affected communities face severe restrictions and limited access to resources,

services and development, keeping most in severe poverty. In India atrocities and violence against Dalits are on a double-digit rise, whereas acquittal rates for these crimes remain extremely high. The attacks are brutal and inhumane, ranging from gang-rapes to the recent burning alive of two children in India's Haryana state.[1]

PK regards caste as a serious disease, like cancer, and discrimination is merely the symptom. We must focus on curing the disease (the root of the problem) rather than the symptom, and love and compassion are the appropriate medicines to do this. In Sanskrit, the word Dalit means 'suppressed, smashed, broken to pieces'. Legislation can achieve only so much. As PK says: 'laws are useless if left unenforced. Ancient prejudices are embedded in people's minds like layers of bedrock. Change must come from within, from the heart.'

1   Human Rights Watch statement: 11 March 2016, General Debate on Ending Discrimination Based on Caste and Descent

PK's Acknowledgments

First of all, I would like to express my deepest gratitude to Juliet, Novin and everyone at Oneworld for their love, warmth and constant support, as well as for their hard work on this story. When I first met them at their publishing house in London I immediately felt at home, and they and all their colleagues have made a great impression on me. As my son commented: 'We have found the best publishing house in the world.' The name 'Oneworld' is very appropriate to their ethos, and we share the same vision for the future of mankind.

This book was born from the story of two individuals, Charlotte and myself. We came from completely different backgrounds, from different continents and different worlds, which eventually became one world! I never dreamed that one day people would be inspired to write, publish and read a book about us.

I would like to thank my mother, who brought me into the world. Although she could not read or write, she was able to use her fingers to count the days, weeks and months, she kept track of Indian tribal festivals and understood the sun, moon and the movements of the planets. My mother taught me how to forgive and how to live in harmony, while my father taught me how to survive. As a child, I spent a lot of time wondering how I could make my mother happy. Today, I can feel her looking down at me from heaven, and I know she is glad that this book has been written about her son.

I am also indebted to Swedish author Per J Andersson and his beloved wife Pernilla for their relentless research over the last six years, during which time Per visited my village in East India and interviewed many of the people mentioned in the book. Special thanks are also due to Liselott and Adam at Forum, and all those involved. I would also like to thank Martin Fletcher for his editorial assistance, and for his postscript on the Indian caste system.

Very special thanks to my dear British friend Anne, who many years ago agreed to type out my old diaries on my typewriter. She felt a strong emotional attachment to my story and gave me a great deal of encouragement, and she is a very loyal friend to me and all my family.

Finally, neither this story nor the book would have been possible without Charlotte's warmth and unconditional love. As well as my wife, life partner and best friend, she is my goddess – I not only love her, but I worship her.

I must also give my deepest thanks to my beloved wife for being infinitely patient with me, for letting me talk endlessly and for listening to all my ideas. Special thanks to our daughter Emelie, a sympathetic soul and a great flute player like my dad, for her true moral support, and to our son, the prince Karl Siddhartha – he is the real businessman of the family and has many other wonderful talents. I am also very grateful to Charlotte's dear mother AnnMarie for her invaluable advice on how to live in the Swedish countryside in an eco-friendly way, and for affectionately calling me Mowgli for the last 40 years, just like my grandfather always did. I am also thankful to Charlotte's sister Ulla who is an excellent horse rider, is always brutally honest, and who has been cutting my hair better than a professional barber since I arrived in Sweden.

Last but not the least, I beg the forgiveness of all those who helped me, fed me and gave me valuable advice during my long overland journey on the hippie trail from the east to the west and whose names I have failed to mention here.

PHOTO ALBUM

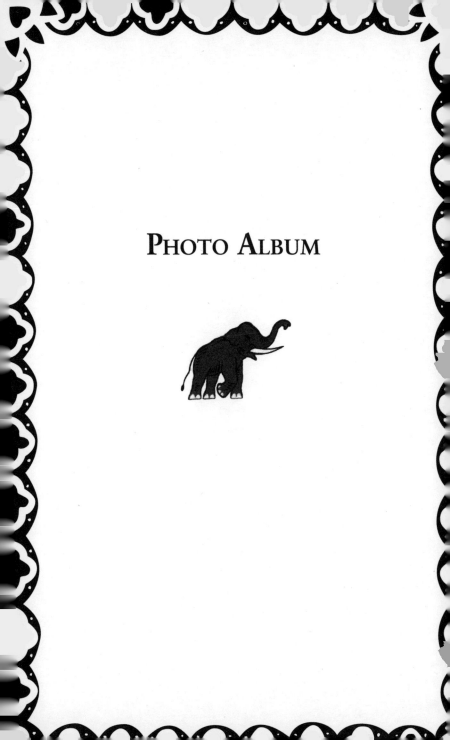

Shridhar, PK's father

PK, standing between his father and mother, with his younger brother Prabir and a cousin sitting in front

Kalabati, PK's mother

Self-portrait entitled 'Love to my Lotta'

A portrait of PK by his friend Tarique

PK doing portraits by Connaught Place in New Delhi

Drawing a Swedish lady

PK meeting the Soviet cosmonaut Valentina Teresjkova, whom he had just drawn

B.D. Jatti was the third president to be drawn by PK in just a few short years

Visiting Prime Minister Indira Ghandi with friends from Orissa

Lotta and a friend in Varanasi

The first photo of PK and Lotta together, taken in
New Delhi in January 1976

PK in his home in New Delhi

PK and Lotta in Lodi Colony in New Delhi

Together again after the long bicycle ride

PK and Lotta's wedding in Borås on 28 May 1979, exactly two years after they were reunited in Sweden

Upside-down yoga at a conference for the blind at Mullsjö College

A Mahanadia-von Schedvin family portrait taken at a studio in Sandared

The family: Emelie, Lotta, PK, Karl-Siddharta

PK and Lotta at home in Kroksjöås

Morning Prayer at a school in Baghmunda, where PK's niece Ranjita is a teacher

PK talks to students at Kalinga Institute of Social Sciences (KISS), Odisha

About PK and Lotta

PK and LOTTA have been happily married since 1979. They have two children and live in Borås, Sweden. PK is an Art and Culture Adviser for the Swedish Government, and also the Oriya Cultural Ambassador to Sweden.

About the Author

PER J ANDERSSON is a writer and journalist. He is the co-founder of travel magazine *Vagabond*, and has been visiting India for the last 30 years.

About the Translator

ANNA HOLMWOOD translates literature from Swedish and Chinese to English.